HOW TO FEEL GOOD

How to Feel Good Naked

Learning to Love the Body You've Got

SHEILA BRIDGE

**MONARCH
BOOKS**

Oxford, UK, and Grand Rapids, Michigan, USA

First published in the UK in 2010 by Monarch Books
(a publishing imprint of Lion Hudson plc),
Wilkinson House, Jordan Hill Road, Oxford OX2 8DR.
Tel: +44 (0)1865 302750 Fax: +44 (0)1865 302757
Email: monarch@lionhudson.com
www.lionhudson.com

ISBN 978-1-85424-928-9

Distributed by:
UK: Marston Book Services Ltd, PO Box 269,
Abingdon, Oxon OX14 4YN;
USA: Kregel Publications, PO Box 2607
Grand Rapids, Michigan 49501.

This book has been printed on paper and board independently certified as having come from sustainable forests.

British Library Cataloguing Data
A catalogue record for this book is available from the British Library.

Printed and bound in the UK by MPG Books.

Dedicated to my beloved Emma

Contents

Preface

It's OK, don't panic! This book is safe. It will not make you feel guilty, it will not beat you over your head about your emotional inadequacies, it will not chastise you for your self-indulgence nor harangue you for your poor dress sense.

This book doesn't plan to make you feel miserable at all! Would it help you to know that it's not being written by a celebrity icon to promote her "secret of success" diet or exercise programme? Mind you, you've probably worked that out already. So let me tell you a bit about the author: she comfort eats when necessary, exercises with gritted teeth (unless it involves fun) and buys most of her clothes in charity shops (writers don't get paid much).

Sheila is the lady I see in the mirror. She is neither a role model nor a success story. She's just an ordinary woman with the usual shed-load of insecurities. On the one hand, she doesn't feel terribly well qualified to write on this subject; on the other, she thinks she's remarkably well informed. Confusion and ambivalence are conditions she is used to. Anyway, she's done her best but couldn't have managed it by herself, the following people are owed far more than the mention they are about to get: Liz Dernie, Sarah Miles, Alison Tinsley, Charlotte Dunkerley, Emma Bridge, Heather McQuillan and Hazel Harrison. Variously they offered unstinting encouragement, excellent proof-reading, thoughtful suggestions and penetrating insights. I'm hoping a fancy coffee and cake of your choice will cover it (see previous comment on earnings) so let's make a date.

So, if you don't like this book, use it to prop up the short leg on your bed, that way it will at least perform some kind of useful function. As for your shape, this book might turn out to be less effective in the short-term than a pair of magic pants but I'm hopeful it will be more encouraging than yet another diet book. I want to reassure you: you are not about to be told that a doughnut should never pass your lips again. This is a book about embracing life, embracing yourself and allowing yourself to be embraced by the source of life and love, your Creator, God himself.

Sheila Bridge

Introduction

At some point in your life you have stood in front of a mirror and said the words, "If only…"

It might have been at the age of eleven when, finding a great top to wear to the school disco, you tried it on and sighed, "If only… I had the boobs to fill it." It might have been at seventeen, lying flat on your bedroom floor, fighting to do up the zip on your tight jeans: "If only… my bum wasn't so big." Or maybe it's been in later life that the "if only"s have crept up on you: "if only I could lose the weight"; "if only my legs were longer"; "if only my feet were smaller".

Ask any group of women to raise their hands if there is one thing they would change about their bodies, and I guarantee that whatever the size of the group, all of them will be able to find something worth fixing. It seems that being dissatisfied with our appearance is a "normal" part of the female experience. And now that beauty therapists offer treatments to both sexes and men's magazines seem just as preoccupied with body image as their female counterparts, maybe this is not just a female concern.

I wonder when we first began to be unhappy about our bodies? There must have been a time in our lives when we were completely careless about how we looked or how we dressed. When we played in the sandpit in not much more than a grubby vest, surely we were happy then; but even just arriving at school brought choices between clothes and colours and, for the girls, issues over plaits or pony-tails. Some woke early to the need to "look good" and others of us, myself included, remained in blissful ignorance (well, ignorance, anyway) till well into our teens.

Most of us can remember feeling awkward about our bodies as teenagers. Boys suddenly find their limbs get too long for their bodies and they become temporarily clumsy. Girls constantly compare themselves to their peers and suffer acute anxiety if they are suddenly too tall or too busty. At around fourteen I had the horrible realization that hairy legs, National Health glasses and wearing beige were doing nothing for me. Beige might look great on you, but it makes me look like a corpse, and it's not a good look with long greasy hair! My personal quest for self-improvement had begun.

Whole industries are built on the basis that we are unhappy about our appearance: fashion, magazines, cosmetics. If we were satisfied with our appearance, authors of diet books would have to have to find something else to write about. Manufacturers of all those strange devices to tighten, flatten or flatter would go out of business, and plastic surgeons would go bust – in the financial sense of that word.

Of course, we're not all obsessed with our appearance. There are some people who just don't care (and you rather wish they did), there are others who care a bit and do a bit about it, and then there are those whose whole lives are dominated by the pursuit of beauty (some of whom hide themselves away because they feel grotesque). Where do you fit in? The fact that you're reading this book probably means you at least care a bit, and possibly it means you actually care a lot. Maybe you also feel a bit guilty about how much you care.

We need to get honest with ourselves, so here's the deal: I'll tell you my hang-ups if you promise to be honest about yours (this is going to get a bit girly for the next paragraph). Here goes.

I've spent a decade of my life being overweight and now that I'm not overweight, I'll admit to being a bit obsessed about staying that way. Motherhood left me with stretch-marks like contour lines round my butt, so I would never be seen on a beach in anything less than a full swimsuit, preferably the variety with shorts. I have eyebrows that would like to meet in the middle and, as a dark-haired woman, I have experienced almost every known method of hair removal. By now I have made myself sound like a shrunken, wrinkled, hairy freak! But believe it or not, I have good bits. I have nice eyes, my teeth are straight and I have tiny, lady-like wrists – elegant wrists are a very difficult feature to make the most of, but believe me, I try. I like to believe I'm not obsessed about my appearance, but put me in front of a group I'd like to impress, and suddenly how I look becomes rather important. Am I a shallow, insecure individual? Or am I just normal?

In my journey towards self-acceptance I have come to two firmly held conclusions. The first is that the desire to be attractive, even beautiful, is a natural and good part of what it means to be female. Adam looked at Eve and saw that she was "good". Well, there's an understatement! I think he looked at Eve and said, "Phoar!" I believe in a Creator God who planted in my inner being a desire to be attractive, to have that kind of impact. Don't worry if you don't take the Adam and Eve story literally: I'd still like you to get hold of the fact

"You know what they say about owners & pets looking alike?
I'd be worried if I was that basset hound!"

"We're not all obsessed with our appearance." (p.12)

that wanting to look good is an OK thing. You don't have to suppress it. Being concerned about your appearance does not make you a shallow human being.

For men there is also a link between how they feel about their bodies and how they feel about themselves. Lots of men find other ways to boost their self-regard and sex appeal, money and power being the main two. As a result they get away with paying scant attention to grooming, presentation and physique (this is why grossly overweight millionaires have no shortage of slim, attractive female companions). Just because men boost their self-esteem in this way doesn't mean to say that men don't ever feel insecure about their bodies. A lot of men do have body-image issues; it's just a lot harder for them to admit it.

My second conclusion is that the secret to being a body beautiful actually lies much deeper than our surface concerns about cellulite, crow's feet, bingo wings or beer bellies. I believe that the best thing we can do towards self-improvement is to change the way we think about ourselves. Diet magazines carry endless stories about people who lose loads of weight and each person says something like, "It's totally changed the way I feel about myself." They've come to value themselves as individuals; they start to respect their bodies; having taken control of their eating, they feel in much greater control of the rest of their lives. I think it's great that they've discovered this new self-respect, but also just kind of sad that they've only discovered this self-confidence through a diet. Maybe if they'd had a deep-down positive view of themselves, they wouldn't have got so overweight in the first place. I wonder if achieving a smaller waist measurement is really the answer to sorting out all those issues.

My belief is that if we really want to be content as individuals, then it's not going to be a diet or an exercise regime that gets us there. These might be helpful things along the way, but the most important thing we can do is sort out the issue of our self-esteem. In other words, we need to feel good about ourselves, whatever shape we are in. Only when we've done that can we find the resolve, courage and self-discipline to get our body working for us, becoming the best that it can be.

My aim with this book is ambitious. I want you to feel at home in your beautiful body, *whatever shape it's in*. Hence the title, a tribute to Gok Wan, whose TV series has done so much to help women of all shapes and sizes to feel good about themselves. You might feel you are too tall, too short, too fat, too thin or too hairy. You may have big feet, short arms, wispy hair, freckles you don't like, too many chins, wonky teeth, big ears, boobs that drop to your waist, eyebrows that meet in the middle, knees that turn in, toes that turn out… whatever! I don't care. I still believe that it's possible to feel good about yourself, whatever shape you're in. Not only is it possible, it's absolutely vital.

This book will help you change your shape if you really think that's necessary. Your body will work better when it's at an ideal weight and it's not abused by overwork, lack of sleep, inadequate diet or lack of exercise. There *are* a few people who reach a truly happy state of self-acceptance with less than perfect physique, and good for them. For the rest of us there is a clear link between our mental state, our emotional state and our physical state, so there's no point pretending to be happy if we feel fat, frumpy or unfit. This book is not about pretending. We need to be honest and realistic: there is a link between how we look and how we feel. So this book will look at why we feel the way we do, help us sort out if those feelings are reasonable and then help us plot a path towards feeling better about ourselves – including the shape we are in.

For many of us the issue is not "Should we be bothered about our appearance?" but "How much should we be bothered about our appearance?" Just how much time, effort or money is it reasonable to spend on being a body beautiful? Is it hollow vanity to pay for plastic surgery if the shape of your nose upsets you? Can you justify expense on hair colour, fake tans and painted nails? Aren't these just shallow preoccupations when half the world lives in rags and doesn't have enough to eat?

When Jesus told his disciples to "Consider how the lilies grow. They do not labour or spin. Yet I tell you, not even Solomon in all his splendour was dressed like one of these" (Luke 12:27) – did he mean we shouldn't give any time, thought or effort to clothes – or did he mean we should aspire to be as beautiful as a "lily"? What place should beauty treatments, fashion concerns and exercise regimes have in our lives? The answers to all these questions are not as obvious as you think. They are not easy questions.

I hope that by the end of the book you'll have found your own answers. I also hope that you'll have looked honestly at your body hang-ups, maybe learnt a bit about your own amazing body and started to speak differently to yourself. Then and only then, if you realize it's really necessary, I hope you can begin a journey of change towards a healthier, better-looking lifestyle, because you – yes, even you – can feel good naked.

Chapter 1

The Pressure to Be Perfect

"Perfect? Me? You've got to be joking!"

"Perfect" is a word we rarely, if ever, apply to ourselves. We use it for others, as in "she has perfect skin" or a "perfect figure", but do we use it to describe ourselves? Not likely. Similarly, we'd far rather tell our friends all the things we feel need changing about our appearance and we are far less likely to comment on the things we actually like about ourselves. We have aspirations for longer legs, flatter tummies, straighter noses, clearer skin… You name it, and we might want to change it. We know we're not "perfect". But that doesn't mean the word doesn't have power over us.

It used to be that any less-than-perfect female could comfortably shrug her shoulders over her shortcomings and think something along the lines of, "Well, I might have a big bum but I've a great smile and gorgeous hair." Nowadays it feels like there is such a huge pressure to be perfect that we are at risk of losing our sense of perspective; we can't see past the "big bum", but not because it's any bigger than before! We seem to have lost our ability to tolerate our shortcomings. I've lost count of the number of times I have spoken to a lovely-looking woman who completely fails to see any of her own redeeming features because she is so distressed over that *one* thing that seems so overwhelmingly repulsive: "too much fat around the tops of my thighs", "flab that wobbles about under my upper arms", "one breast larger than the other". Sometimes I feel like shouting at them, "Look at you! You are gorgeous! You are amazing! Honestly, no one even notices the problem that you are so upset about."

But these women can't hear me. They are sold on perfection. They've been made to believe it's achievable, if they just try hard enough, or save up enough money for the surgery. They are deaf to any good news about their looks, because they have become convinced they are deeply unattractive.

Unfortunately, these women are not rare; in fact, the way they feel about their bodies is so "everyday", it is virtually normal. "These women" are not an extreme bunch of celebrity slaves or fashionistas. "These women" are you, me, my friends, your friends, our daughters, the girl next door, the young girls on the bus, the women in any high street. A survey for *Grazia*[1] magazine found that an astonishing 98 per cent of women "hate" their bodies and that the average British woman worries about her body every fifteen minutes. Apparently seven out of ten said their lives would improve if they had "better" bodies.

Of course, you could argue that readers of *Grazia* magazine would say that, wouldn't they? Surely more than 2 per cent of the female population feel good enough about themselves not to be bothered to reply to a questionnaire on body image? I'd like to think so, but there are heaps of other studies that indicate we have reached a very unhappy state of affairs between ourselves and our bodies.

How did it get to be like this? Why are women generally so down on themselves? Maybe we should blame it on a culture which treats women as sex objects. For a night out with colleagues, a lap-dancing club may now be considered as reasonable an option as a night-club, a show or a casino. Supermarkets sell T-shirts for ten-year-old girls with slogans such as "so many boys, so little time". Increased sexualization certainly sends out the message that a woman's worth lies in her attractiveness. However, I think women themselves must take part of the blame.

We are our own worst enemies. It's the *women's* magazines that sell perfection and obsess over size, diet and cellulite. These magazines are underpinned by the notion that appearance is everything. I even found a headline above a fashion article that proclaimed, "It's what's on the outside that counts"! "No, it isn't!" I wanted to shout. We are being sold a lie. It is "perfect-looking" women who sell us everything from "age perfect" face-cream (how ironic) to hair dye to cover the grey, "because we're worth it". Their seeming perfection is a lie: there are *no* women who look as good as they do in advertisements. We have forgotten what normal women look like.

The other recent feature of women's magazines is that they now gleefully publish photos of celebrities looking less than their best, joyfully highlighting their shortcomings. So a star might have "chunky thighs" or be "scarily skinny" or find themselves criticized for having "sweaty armpits" or "hairy legs" (doesn't *everyone* have these?). At first sight this might seem to reassure us – after all, even celebrities have off days. But actually this type of article raises the bar even higher, because of the way we women think. Some of us will gleefully gloat over someone else's fat thighs, but in reality all of us end up thinking about our own thighs, fat or not. All that happens is that we become more self-conscious, not less. There is a train of thought that runs: "Well, if *she* can't look good all the time, what hope do I have?"

So we can't win. We see perfection and it depresses us. We see normality and it repulses us. Either way, we end up with negative feelings about our bodies.

Self-loathing has become "a default position for the average female", comments Carol Midgley.[2] "Declaring yourself totally happy with your looks and figure just isn't done. It means you are smug. Or deluded. Or possibly mad."[3]

There's even a word for all this negative talk: "bodysnarking",[4] the practice of making snide, cruel, pointed remarks about another woman's appearance. TV programmes like *America's Next Top Model, Extreme Makeover* and *Ten Years Younger* all encourage women to watch critically from their sofas and comment freely on the physical imperfections of women on the screen. Bodysnarking is also on the internet. Websites like Hotornot.com invite individuals to post up photos of themselves so that their attractiveness can be rated. Other people's flaws and assets can be obsessively scrutinized, which might seem fair game: after all, they chose to go on the programme or post up a photo. But this bodysnarking simply increases the insecurity of those who watch.

By being negative about other women, we actually become more critical of ourselves. We have lost the ability to speak positively about ourselves. We have lost the shock value of harsh-sounding phrases such "muffin top", "bingo wings" or "whale tail". Where once it was considered rude to comment on someone's appearance, today it seems that anyone can say anything they want.

Blogs mean that anyone can express an opinion and a less-than-flattering photo of you can be forwarded to the world in minutes on Facebook, Flickr, Twitter or Tumblr.

In 2008 Anna Holmes, the editor in chief of a blog called *Jezebel*, posted "This Year, Let's Call it Quits on The Nasty Nitpicking",[5] a resolution aimed at changing the way young women talk about each other. A good sentiment, but she's too late. Teenagers always could be incredibly cruel in the remarks they made to one another, but now, in the ironically faceless interactions on Facebook, they can be even more uninhibited in their comments.

In her book *Bodies* Susie Orbach writes that it is "now *so ordinary* to be distressed about our bodies or body parts that we dismiss the gravity of body problems"[6] (emphasis mine).

Perfection has not just been sold in adverts. It has also been sold to us on the catwalks. In 1975 models weighed only 8 per cent less than the average woman. By 1997 they weighed 23 per cent less, a size achievable by less than 5 per cent of the population.[7] The "tyranny of thinness" has continued with a major supermarket chain introducing a mainstream fashion range with clothes that go down to size 0 (UK size 4). Have you ever wondered just how small that is? The typical waist measurement of a size-0 skirt is 22 inches or 55 centimetres, which should be the waist size for a healthy eight-year-old girl! That is *so* mad, I don't know whether to laugh or cry. On balance it makes me want to cry. Knowing that an American survey revealed that 81 per cent of ten year olds are so afraid of being fat that they have already tried to diet, and that 54 per cent of women would rather be hit by a truck than be fat (yes, you read that right),[8] it seems to me that the pressure to be perfect is leaving millions of women lost in a desperate state of self-loathing.

We have an idea about what perfection looks like, but this is mostly based on air-brushed images of people we've never met in the flesh, people who've not only had an unfair share from the good-looking end of the gene pool but also the services of stylists, image enhancers and personal trainers. We know it's outrageous that celebrities might pay more for one hair-do than we'd spend on groceries in a month, but even so, we buy into the idea of perfection.

Of course, some of us are more driven by it than others. Most of us don't like to admit that we are unduly influenced by culture or advertising, but none of us are immune. Maybe you are reading this thinking, "I'm completely at home with my imperfections" – and if that's the case, good for you! But there

"Does my bolt look big in this?"

"I'm completely at home with my imperfections." (p.20)

is a woman near you, someone you love, maybe your daughter, your sister, your friend, someone whose life experiences and self-confidence are being sapped by this constant pressure to be perfect, or by their own constant sense of failure. Or maybe you did pick this book up for yourself. On a scale where "10" means you are obsessive about your appearance and "1" means you really don't worry at all, where would you put yourself? Somewhere in the middle, I'm guessing, but probably more to one side or the other. Most of us are prepared to admit that we are at least a little uncomfortable about some part of our anatomy. We are somewhere between the two extremes: there are some things we like but there are other things we'd change if we could. There are some things we feel comfortable about doing to improve our appearance (tidy eyebrows/shave armpits/brush our hair) but other things would feel extreme. The tricky thing is that what feels extreme for one person seems totally acceptable to the next. So is a leg wax reasonable but a boob job obsessive? How far should you go with personal grooming? How much is it "reasonable" to spend? If the problem is sapping your self-confidence, is *any* price too high to pay the plastic surgeon, or is there an alternative way to boost your self-esteem?

The risk about taking expensive and extreme measures to "solve" whichever physical shortcoming bothers you the most is that even when the problem is "fixed", will your heart be satisfied? Will you *then* be content with who you are and how you look? Will you really be freed to take your eyes off yourself and enjoy loving and being loved by those around you?

I would love to revisit those participants of shows like *Extreme Makeover* one year down the line, because I have a nagging feeling that all the insecurity that made them feel so negative about themselves in the first place might have re-emerged. I don't think you can fix up the outside, the façade, the appearance of a person, and expect that to so totally change their feelings about themselves that they never feel unhappy again. If you don't ever take a look on the inside and unpack all the self-loathing that got in there in the first place and replace that with a deep-down self-acceptance and a sense of being unconditionally loved, then no amount of surface rearrangement will ever be enough. By the end of this book I hope to point to what I believe to be the only reliable route to self-acceptance and the richest source of unconditional love.

So the challenge facing us is "How can we feel good about ourselves when there will always be something that disappoints?" If we want to change our appearance, how far should we go? Exercise? Diet? Fake a tan? Pluck your eyebrows? Dye your hair? What if we still don't feel good after all these efforts? What then? Fashion makeover? Cosmetic surgery? Will any of these things bring about the positive feelings we long for, and even with any expensive self-enhancement, is it possible to ever *really* feel good naked?

These are the questions that I hope to address in the course of this book. By the end of our walk through the worlds of diet, exercise and fashion, I hope to have shown you just how much pressure you are under, to give you some easy ways to feel good about your body and finally to point you to a reliable source of unconditional love.

The bad news behind the "good news"

Newsagents' shelves wouldn't be stocked full of magazines like *Closer*, *Cosmopolitan* or *GQ* if they didn't sell. Pick up almost any of them and 101 seemingly positive messages will leap out at you from the front cover: promises for "Instant glamour"; how to have a "Flatter stomach forever"; how to "Recharge your love life", "Kick start your energy the natural way" or "Make earning fun". All of these hold out a hope for self-improvement in some area of your life: social, physical, material or relational. All sound like "good news" stories.

But behind the headlines there is an insidious message. The message is: "You don't have to be tired, stressed, unhealthy, unattractive, or unfriendly – just follow our simple advice and you too can be full of energy, confidence, ambition, bursting with health, enjoying your good looks, juggling a successful career and living in complete harmony with all your nearest and dearest." Yeah, right, who are they kidding?

Behind all this "simple" advice and appealing headlines is a sinister, negative, life-threatening message. This message is poisonous to your self-esteem. Listen to it often enough and it will prove deadly. Put simply, the message is this: *You are inadequate.* You are failing in some shape or form. Maybe you're too fat, maybe you're too ugly, maybe your dress sense is unacceptable; whatever it is, *you are inadequate.* It's hardly surprising that most of us feel too fat after a dip into a magazine. In recent studies, even brief exposure to magazine photographs of super-thin models makes us feel depressed, stressed, guilty, shameful, insecure and less satisfied with our own bodies.[9] And we are bombarded with images of what Naomi Woolf calls "The Official Body" – an idealized image of female beauty – so often, in fact, that exceptional good looks seem normal and anything short of the ideal seems abnormal and ugly.[10]

If you are a mother wondering why your daughter is so obsessed with her appearance, it might help you to know that young women today see more images of outstandingly beautiful women in one day than you did throughout your entire adolescence.[11] It's no good blaming her for being vain or self-obsessed; you need to understand the pressure on her from every angle. It's been estimated that the average person sees between 2,000 and 5,000 digitally altered images of bodies or faces per week.[12] Let's not even use the euphemism "enhanced". These pictures tell outright lies. Take a look at before and after films of photo shoots, and you will see an ordinary girl with lank hair and poor skin transformed into a cover girl.[13] The camera *always* lies.

Even if you steer clear of magazines, you are still going to get the same message from the wider world. On television there are whole programmes devoted to reducing our weight as a nation. There are makeover shows that will guide you through the more extreme end of self-improvement: body sculpture by surgery as well as the more "normal" transformations effected by hair extensions, teeth whitening or eyebrow shaping. Very rude television presenters will tell you "what not to wear"; other programmes will tell you how to decorate your home, arrange your garden or prepare your meals, all in ways that will "enhance your lifestyle". All of these programmes work on the basic assumption that your lifestyle needs enhancing. In other words, you are inadequate.

This message is so pervasive that we almost fail to recognize it. It's whispered to us in adverts, hinted at in films full of idealized romance and blasted full volume off the covers of most women's magazines. The drip-drip effect of this negative message is that our confidence is undermined, our self-esteem is sapped and we do indeed feel ourselves to be in need of all the self-improvement therapy we can get. We have come to believe it: we *are* inadequate.

The truth is, we are not. There is no such thing as an ordinary person. Everyone you have ever clapped eyes on has an incredible body that functions in amazingly diverse ways, keeping that person alive. Everyone has a talent, a gift. Everyone has a personality; preferences for one thing or another that mark them out as unique. Everyone has at least one attractive feature, most have many, even if not all those features are physical. People have passions, interests or hobbies that turn them into experts in particular areas. Some people have abilities that make them stand out; they are gifted musicians, mathematicians or microbiologists. Others have compassionate and sensitive hearts that allow them to serve others in ways that give dignity and respect. All of these qualities are what makes up one individual. Yet if you believed the media message, you would come away thinking that being slim, sexy and attractive are the only true measures of a person's worth.

Our culture feeds us four lies in the race for perfection: "Be Beautiful" and "Be Famous" are favourites. If you can't manage those, then strive to "Be Busy and Be Successful". At the very least, "Be Busy". If we not one or all of these four things, then social shipwreck looms.

Be Beautiful

When Renée Zellweger made the second film for the *Bridget Jones* series, she had to put on some weight to play the central character. As the film came out, naturally many magazines and newspapers ran interviews with its star actress. Of all the questions that she was asked, the one that came up over and over again, the one on which most articles focused, was the issue of weight gain and loss. How had she gained all that weight and then lost it again, apparently without effort? Did she look better at size 16 than size 12? How did she feel about her larger self? Renée herself found this fascination with the weight issue rather tedious. Never mind that as an American actress she had faultlessly delivered a completely convincing English accent. Never mind that she had been faithful to the character as created by the original writer, never mind any of her many other achievements in the film – it seemed that all people were interested in was her weight.

Women seem to be judged on their appearance far more than men. One large business recently courted controversy because it held a workshop offering advice on "self-presentation" and dress sense for its female staff. Why weren't its male employees being trained to improve their "self-presentation"? Female newsreaders have not been kept on for as long as their male counterparts, as if their journalistic or delivery skills have been impaired by the ageing process.

Unless you work in radio, it seems that your ability to do your job is somehow connected to your ability to look good. And with a few rare exceptions, looking good is equated with looking thin. Tessa Jowell, the UK Culture Secretary, in 2007 said, "Fashion and the tyranny of thinness can undermine the self-confidence of young women", but her views have largely gone unheard. Although some fashion weeks in places like Milan and Madrid have introduced regulations about minimum age and size for models, many others have no regulations, only suggesting that super-skinny very young models should be discouraged. As Michael Gove comments, the effect of this is that "For all women – and especially teenagers – who cannot squeeze into a size 0 without either starvation or surgery, the images the fashion industry sell are invitations to self-loathing."[14]

The problem starts young. In the twelve months from February 2008, 200,000 girls in the UK between nine and sixteen played the Miss Bimbo beauty contest game online. Each participant starts with a naked virtual character. The aim is to win "bimbo" dollars to buy sexy outfits and send your character out clubbing. In order to progress in the game you must strive to become "the most famous, beautiful, sought after bimbo across the globe". Along the way your character can be kept at her target weight through diet pills, enhance her appearance with plastic surgery and date a famous "hottie". You can imagine what these young girls are learning about their value from such a "game".

No wonder 74 per cent of girls in the UK are so dissatisfied with their bodies that they would like to change something about their appearance. This figure rises to 92 per cent for those aged fifteen to seventeen.[15] This phenomenon is not confined to the UK. Over ten years ago an American survey found that 81 per cent of ten-year-old girls had already dieted at least once. In Sweden 25 per cent of seven year olds had dieted to lose weight, and in Japan 41 per cent of elementary school girls (some as young as six) thought they were too fat.[16] I don't know about you, but when I was aged six or ten, chocolate mini-roll cakes were the best thing ever, I was playing with baby dolls, not bimbos, and I would sooner have flown to the moon than go on a diet.

Wallis Simpson, the American socialite, twice divorced, who married the heir to the British throne in 1936, once said, "You can never be too rich or too thin." This is not a witty observation: it is a black lie. In 2006 two size-0 models, one in Brazil and one in Uruguay, died from conditions related to their fragile weight. Dr Dee Dawson, one of the UK's leading experts on eating disorders, describes the effect of mainstream retailers selling size-0 clothes: "the only grown up people who can wear this size are people who are ill. It's not natural... when you have the equivalent of size 0 on the racks this normalises this idea of being ultra-thin."[17]

Not every culture cultivates such a degree of self-loathing. In 2008 a survey in Spain revealed that 60 per cent of Spanish women are completely content with the way they look.[18] So what's going on there? According to *Grazia* magazine, the UK figure is 2 per cent! A discussion on *Woman's Hour* suggested a number of factors: young girls in Spain are brought up in a strong family culture which places a high value on "vocal cherishing". In other words, little girls are appreciated verbally. Far from being reticent about compliments, Spanish families enthusiastically tell their girls that they are are *"bonita"* or a *"preciosa chiquita"* (pretty, precious girl) from an early age. And, lo and behold, the girls grow up believing it. Spanish women are not objectively any more or less attractive than women anywhere else. They just believe they are better looking! They also have a wider range of feminine role models in their culture and take some pride in a more voluptuous look. Penelope Cruz was made to wear a prosthetic bottom for one of her Spanish films because she was considered too skinny. Given that half the cabinet ministers in Spain at the time of this research were female[19] no wonder they were one of the first countries to introduce legislation to the catwalks regarding the size of models.

Further evidence that women are susceptible to this media-imported, narrow definition of female physical beauty was found on the island of Fiji where there was no access to TV until 1995. Just three years later the incidence of bulimia had rocketed as young girls tried to get their bodies to look like the westernised characters they saw on TV.[20]

Be Famous

A recent survey in a UK school reported fears that children's obsessions with footballers, pop stars and actors were affecting their progress in school and limiting their career aspirations.[21] Apparently one third of the children interviewed just wanted to be "famous". Elizabeth Farrar, a primary school teacher, said too many pupils believed academic success was "unnecessary" because they thought they would be able to make their fame and fortune quite easily on a reality TV show. Whilst good role models such as sportsmen and sportswomen do clearly give a healthy living message, a lot of the more lurid headlines could be said to encourage under-age drinking and anti-social behaviour. A large number of girls surveyed thought that Paris Hilton was a good role model. Paris Hilton! Famous for being famous. Not, as far as I'm aware, a person who's championed any great cause, invented any life-changing cure or even attempted any awe-inspiring challenge. She has, however, served a custodial sentence for a drink-driving conviction. No offence, Paris, but I'm heart-broken if you are the best we can offer our daughters.

In America an estimated 250,000 babies, toddlers and young children take part in beauty pageants. *Toddlers and Tiaras* is a weekly reality show on *The Learning Channel*. Personally I think toddlers are gorgeous and always look cute but the toddlers on this programme appear to need a lot of help in looking good. They wear false eyelashes, spray on tans, have manicured fingernails and even shaven legs. This is outrageous. It is exploitation and sexualisation at its most extreme. There has been a growing outcry lead by two female high school students to get this programme off the air. In a similar way a UK mainstream store caused outrage when they sold an all in one vest for babies aged 3 months with the slogan "Does my bum look big in this?"

It seems that celebrity status is mainly about looks and the ability to self-publicize. In 2006 Mia Rose uploaded videos of herself singing on YouTube and bagged herself a record deal, becoming the eighth most subscribed musician of all time on YouTube.[22] Kate Nash and Lily Allen also started on MySpace, and Lily's song entitled "The Fear" opens with a statement that being rich is much more important than being either intelligent or pleasant. By the end of the song she is completely disorientated in a mixed-up world where film stars matter more than mothers and being thin is the most important thing of all.

Maybe this song is meant to be highly ironic, a send-up of the shallowness of celebrity culture, but personally I think it expresses only too clearly the empty promise that happiness would be within our grasp if only we could get famous. James Morrison sang, "I'm not lost… just undiscovered." I think a whole generation of young women will remain disappointed that they've never been "discovered", and as a consequence, unless they find some better way to feel good about themselves, they will feel "lost".

So what's the answer? How can we be happy, sane, well-balanced women when we are under so much pressure from the world around? Should we reject the whole "women should look good" idea entirely? Should we live in the fashion equivalent of a sack, eat chocolate and doughnuts without regret and refuse any form of self-grooming? (That's a bit too extreme for some of us, I fear. Within a month I'd look like an ape, actually it might not take that long.) Or should we move to one of the places in the world where they value big women? In Jamaica or Nigeria fat is seen as a sign of prosperity and fertility. But even there we would find thin women buying pills to bulk themselves up and young girls being force fed in "fattening rooms". Even though in these places women seem to be after different things – to be fat rather than thin – in reality the tyranny of being defined, accepted or rejected on the basis of your body shape is exactly the same.

We could move to Brazil where apparently you can get a government-funded breast enhancement to save you from having low self-esteem. Paying to have implants stuffed under women's skin is apparently cheaper than psychotherapeutic help.[23] In other words, who cares about what's going on in your head or about the mad messages the world is giving you concerning what you "ought" to look like? Just lie down on the table, count slowly to ten and someone will rearrange your assets!

There has to be a better way. None of us can get away from our bodies. The only choice we have is to "get away" from the pressures and messages that bombard us. Changing the way we think about ourselves is a much longer-term project than changing our body shape or size, but in my view it will, in the long run, be far more beneficial. If at the moment every "encounter" with your body, either in the mirror, in a changing room, or puffing up the stairs, is an occasion for self-criticism or self-loathing, then what chance do you ever stand of feeling good? All you will ever feel is a drive towards self-improvement or a sense of misery over your lack of self-discipline. We need to find a way of changing every encounter with our bodies into a moment of celebration: *I'm alive, I'm amazing, I have limbs that move, a heart that beats, eyes that see, skin that feels, arms that hug, lips that smile, a brain that works.* Nina Simone sings some brilliant lyrics in her song "Ain't Got No, I Got Life".[24] First she lists, blues style, all the things she hasn't got, then the chorus lifts to a wonderful celebration of all she's got that "nobody can take away": her hair, her head, her brains, her ears, her eyes, nose, mouth, smile, tongue, chin, neck, boobies, heart, soul, back and sex!

Some of us will give up in the face of these first two pressures to "Be Beautiful" or "Be Famous", but others will find two more pressures or directives that seem to offer their own route to self-acceptance and satisfaction.

Notes

1.   *Grazia* magazine, April 2006.
2.   Carol Midgley, "Women are their own worst enemies", *The Times*, 7 August 2008.
3.   Ibid.
4.   Hannah Seligson, "The Rise of Bodysnarking", *Wall Street Journal Online*, 16 May 2008: http://online.wsj.com/article/SB121089779322097255.html.
5.   Ibid.
6.   Susie Orbach, *Bodies*, UK: Profile Books, 2009.
7.   Kate Fox, *Mirror Mirror: A Summary of Research Findings on body image*, Social Issues Research Centre (SIRC), 1997.
8.   http://www.bodyimageprogram.org/ – Tri Delta press release on http://anybody.squarespace.com.
9.   Kate Fox, *Mirror Mirror*.
10.   Ibid.
11.   Ibid.
12.   Hamish Pringle and Peter Field, *Brand Immortality*, London: Kogan Page, 2008.
13.   One such example is the film *Evolution* on the Dove website: www.campaignrealbeauty.co.uk
14.   British MP Michael Gove, *The Times*, 23 February 2009.
15.   Research commissioned by the Campaign for Real Beauty, reported by Sean Poulter, *Daily Mail*, 3 February 2007.
16.   Kate Fox, *Mirror Mirror*.
17.   Sean Poulter, "Asda condemned over plans for a new size zero fashion range", *Daily Mail*, 3 February 2007.
18.   Reported on *Woman's Hour*, February 2008.
19.   As of February 2007.
20.   *British Journal of Psychiatry* Vol 180, June 2002 pp. 509–14
21.   Survey for the Association of Teachers and Lecturers, March 2008.
22.   www.need2know.co.uk
23.   Susie Orbach, *Bodies*.
24.   James Rado and Gerome Ragni, "Aint Got No, I Got Life", Song BMG Music.

Chapter 2

Two More Lies

In 2009 an unknown, unmarried and unemployed 47-year-old woman from Scotland called Susan Boyle shot to fame by taking part in a TV talent contest. Within days of her performance, the video clip of her singing "I Dreamed a Dream" had been viewed by 25 million people around the world on YouTube, and yet this woman didn't even own a computer!

Why did her performance have such an impact? Partly because, as soon as she began to sing, it became clear that she had an amazing voice, partly because she sang an emotional song about having a dream, but mostly because she just didn't look like a star. It was her very obvious ordinariness that lulled the audience into thinking, "Here comes another deluded individual with an unrealistic belief in her own ability." In the newspapers following her performance she was described as having the eyebrows of a Roman emperor, and she said herself that she looked like a garage! She was the type of middle-aged woman who sits behind you on the bus into town and you barely notice her. She didn't have the walk, she didn't have the dress sense, she didn't have the hair, the face or the figure, but, oh boy, did she have the voice!

What Susan's story tells us is that we have come to expect that talent will come in a certain package. Her story links strongly to the two pressures to be beautiful and be famous that we looked at in the first chapter. Given that she's not "beautiful" (at least not by conventional standards) does she deserve to be famous? This is the intriguing question posed by her story. It seems that it is no

"And here to size up our talent tonight
is our lovely hostess"

longer simply enough for someone to have an extraordinary voice; they must also look the part. If you'd closed your eyes throughout the video clip, you'd still be impressed by her voice; it would be no less good. So why are her looks (or lack of them) so much a part of her story? Why do we *not* expect middle-aged people with bushy eyebrows and frumpy hair to have an extraordinary talent? Why shouldn't they?

As I said in the first chapter, you have never laid your eyes on an ordinary person. Every single person on the planet is unique, a "one off", a masterpiece. If that sounds an outrageously arrogant thing to say, I don't mean it in the sense that everyone should be a celebrity. I mean that each person has been uniquely created, brought into being for a reason; they are not an accident, not a random collections of genes, hormones and chemicals. I believe each of us has a purpose, that there are answers to the questions, "Why are we here?" and "Who am I?"

If we don't have satisfactory answers to these questions then we will have a shaky sense of identity. We have already looked at the big lies that say that being beautiful can make us feel significant and being famous can make us feel secure. In this chapter we are going to look at two more big lies, the ones that say being incredibly busy or being a success will give you all the self-worth you need.

Being busy or being successful will definitely give you a great deal of self-worth. Our confidence always increases when we are gainfully employed and there's nothing wrong with that, but is that all there is to self-worth? What if you're not successful? What if you're unemployed or only able to work in a dead-end job that doesn't thrill you? Where do you go then for your sense of self-worth?

Before we get stuck into that, please humour me for a moment and picture in your mind a sturdy three-legged wooden stool. I want to just say a bit more about your identity. This wooden stool that you are imagining represents your identity, your sense of who you are. You can sit securely on it but only if all the legs are present and preferably all equal in length. The three "legs" that support this sense of yourself are: self-worth, significance and security. Virtually all of us left childhood with insufficient quantities of one or other of these factors. Some parents are more to blame than others, but none of us had perfect parents so at least one of the "legs" for our identity is too short and we wobble. Pretty much all of what we do as adults is designed to compensate for that shortfall.

So we get qualifications to make us significant, earn money to make us feel secure and bolster our self-worth with self-enhancement. Intrinsically there is nothing wrong with doing any of those things, but what happens to someone who can't attain them? To put it bluntly: what hope have you got if you are unqualified, unattractive and unemployed? There has to be something else that will give us a secure sense of identity in spite of the challenges we face, and I believe there is: unconditional love is the only thing that can give us a this stable and reliable sense of identity.

Now I have to be upfront with you: for me, it has been a relationship with God as Creator and Father that has provided this reliable source of unconditional love in my life. You many not even have noticed so far that I have been writing from that perspective and I do realise that for many people the very idea of a relationship with God might seem very odd. After all, you might say, "what does God have to do with my life or my hang-ups? What is God like anyway? And how would I ever begin to form a relationship with him?" Those are all very good questions which I'm going to look at in more detail in the final chapter. For now I need to explain that my definition of who I am, my identity and my belief as to why I matter is all tied up in this relationship with God.

Sometimes in life we are given a piece of information that totally changes how we see ourselves, for good or bad. For example, imagine finding out that your mother tried to terminate her pregnancy when she was carrying you. Such a discovery would totally upend all the memories you had of a happy childhood. Or imagine discovering the man you thought was your father wasn't actually your father. Or that you have half-siblings you've never met. Any of these facts would be deeply shocking and distressing, *if* they turned out to be true.

What if I were to give you some positive information about yourself and it turned out to be true? The information that has most helped me live with or overcome my personal imperfections, inadequacies and failings has been the information God gives about me (and you, and all human beings) in his word, the Bible. So for example, he says he created me in my mother's womb, he says he knew about me before he created the world, he says I am part of his "handiwork", he says he loves me so much that he sings over me. He also says that he can forgive all the things that have ever made me ashamed, the things I regret, the ways that I've failed. He says he has a purpose for me, things that he's prepared in advance for me to do. He says he holds my whole life in his hands and I don't have to worry about a thing, because he knows what I need.[1]

If you've never heard that *this* is what God says about you, or if you've never believed it or felt it was relevant to you, then I'd like to invite you to at least pretend for a moment. Ask yourself: "what if all those things in the paragraph above *were* actually true?" How a big an impact would it have on your life if this information was true about you?

How good would that be?

Too good to be true? Personally I don't think so, but we'll come back to why I think they are believable in the final chapters.

Meanwhile, let's continue to look at the pressures that affect us. So far we've looked at the pressure to "Be Beautiful" and to "Be Famous". These are the first two of the four big lies that our culture feeds to us. The next two lies are "Be Busy" and "Be Successful". If you feel you don't make the "Beautiful" grade and you haven't yet become "Famous" as a "mum-turned-blogger" or a "writer/singing superstar/business genius", then you may be tempted to express your significance through either your diary or your bank balance.

Being busy or being successful, but preferably both, seems to be the next best thing to being beautiful. If you can't achieve the latter, at least one of the former is accessible to all. Many aspire to a simpler, quieter lifestyle, but for most of us, like it or not, being busy is a way of life. And maybe that's not a bad thing in itself, except when what we do becomes the sole expression of who we are. When we are merely the sum of all our activities, we have lost the essence of ourselves.

I am often aware, when I meet people for the first time, that the question "What do you do?" is shallow and inadequate for getting to the heart of who they are. It will only tell me so much about them, and yet from whatever response they make to that question, I will inevitably form an opinion about their level of education, their possible income, their status and maybe even their personality traits: so a nurse will be caring, an accountant will be boring, a manual worker may have low literacy levels. But all of these assumptions could be wrong. All I have actually asked is, "How do you make your living?" I haven't yet explored who they are, how they react, what they enjoy or what really matters to them.

For many people, the questions I referred to earlier, such as "Who am I?" or "What am I here for?" are simply too difficult to answer. If you lack a sense of identity or intrinsic value, the easiest way to make up for that emptiness is to be busy or successful, to pile up toys or titles so that your possessions and your business card can become an expression of who you are. These twin pressures also have an impact on the way we use our bodies and how we feel about our bodies.

Be Busy

The pressure to "Be Busy" is all about lifestyle: in addition to holding down a job (which is a given), we might also be expected to have a fulfilling hobby, take regular exercise, learn a second language, eat a balanced diet, keep up with culture, bring up well-balanced kids, exfoliate regularly and floss. Yeah, right! How is all that possible in a regular day?

Apparently, since 1998 the number of people in the UK working more than sixty hours a week has more than doubled. Around a quarter of people employed work more than sixty hours a week. The average number of hours for people in full-time work is around forty-four hours a week, which is the highest figure in the European Union.[2]

Australians now work the longest hours in the developed world. A survey asked Australians recently how much more money it would take for them to be happy. The universal reply, regardless of whether they were on a low, medium or high income, was that they would be happy if they earned one third more.[3] The fact that a lot of them are not "happy" now is evidenced by the fact that one fifth of Australians have experienced "emotional distress".[4] In the UK two thirds of people with annual incomes over £35,000 still felt they could not afford to buy everything they really needed, and even 40 per cent of those earning over £50,000 felt they couldn't afford their needs. Put these statistics together with information that in the UK 25 per cent of us have experienced "emotional distress" in the last twelve months and another 25 per cent of us are on the verge of doing so,[5] and you have a picture of a stressed-out and over-worked society which has forgotten how to be content with little and feels under constant pressure to work harder, earn more and buy more.

When a better body is one of those things that you can buy – a tummy tuck, a breast enhancement or some liposuction – then it's easy to see how controlling our physique can come to be seen as a need ("I *must* do this") rather than a want ("I would like to do this but I can manage if I can't").

More and more women are under pressure, both financially and socially, to return to work as soon as their maternity leave is over. Perhaps this is because society causes them to undervalue the contribution they are making to the emotional well-being of their child or children. If society doesn't seem to value them in this role, they themselves can hardly be blamed for feeling a lack of self-worth as a stay-at-home mum. But the pressure isn't just social, it's also financial. There is a mortgage to be paid and maybe a career to be pursued. After all, what has been the point of taking all those exams from an early age if they are not using their education to an economic advantage? It seems to me that people now rarely achieve academic success simply for the joy of learning for its own sake, but only for the "joy" of earning in a higher-status job.

Be Successful

In terms of "being successful", the pressure is on from a very young age. Children are scored and ranked, it seems, from nursery school to university. Not only is there pressure to get the top grades in exams, there is the pressure to get into the best schools, which might then give better access to the better universities. In westernized societies there has been a hard-fought battle for girls to be given the right to be educated and the opportunity to contribute equally in society. But it has not been without a price. Girls now experience a double pressure. It's not enough to be brainy or clever; you still have to be slim and attractive. It's a rare woman who can feel completely appreciated for her ability apart from her appearance. For our daughters this has led to unprecedented pressure. Between 1987 and 1999 in the UK girls began to out-perform boys in almost every academic subject at every educational stage, but during the same period levels of distress such as depression, anxiety, eating disorders and self-harming rose alarmingly.[6]

High-achieving girls with perfectionist tendencies from well-off families seem the most susceptible. When an A grade as opposed to an A* grade is a cause of lasting distress and shame, something is going very badly wrong. In a survey amongst female students at an Oxford University college, over one third had suffered an eating disorder in their lives. That's a large proportion of intelligent, educated young women with serious body-hatred issues.[7] It seems that young girls whose emotional well-being is pinned on being successful and being attractive are very vulnerable to serious mental imbalance when one or other possibility seems beyond their grasp.

Be Busy and Successful and Let Everyone Know

As if all this wasn't enough, now that we live in a virtual world as well as the real world, there is a whole new layer added to this pressure to be busy and successful. It isn't enough to be actually busy or socially successful; you need to be *seen* to be having a great time by posting up your activities for all your friends to see on your Facebook or MySpace page. In fact you can be so busy doing all that posting, commenting and uploading of photographs that I'm wondering how anyone actually has the time to be out there doing the stuff in the first place. "I'm making socks", "I'm walking in the Peak District", "I'm writing a book". Part of me wants to say, "Well, just go do it then. Why stop and tell everyone?" But I'm not quite such a luddite: those were actually recent posts of mine!

I am a late convert to social networking on the internet. Like many people of my age, it has been my teenage children who have introduced me to this whole new way of relating, and I enjoy many of the useful and fun aspects. But I have often reflected on the pressure this way of relating brings. It's a pressure to be seen to be having a good time. For younger users, it seems like just as soon as you go to that party, take that ski trip or run that half marathon dressed as a Teletubby, the photos have to be posted up. It's as if we don't just have experiences and absorb them or even be absorbed by them, we are under pressure to report them to our friends. I can understand dad filming the child running the three-legged race on sports day, but another part of me wants to say to him, "Put the camera down, clap, cheer and yell the kid on. Maybe you'll revisit the memory in your mind more times than you'll watch the clip on your phone." It feels like we have lost the ability to be in the moment without feeling the need to report or record the moment.

The other effect of social networking sites is that we live in the public eye much more than ever before. This involves a new skill of "filtering": we filter information by making choices between what we are happy for anyone to know about us and personal stuff, and we need to remember that others in our network are making the same choices. But sometimes we forget this, so other

"...and in breaking news from the MyTwitface bloggers -
our celebrity is just pulling out of the station"

"The need to report the moment." (p.38)

people's lives begin to sound rather too "perfect" and we feel intimidated. We might be told online that a friend is doing a charity fund-raiser but never know the deep grief and loss that motivate it. We might hear that someone's child has gained a degree but never know that he's also battling with drugs. We hear that Susie is fabulous at ballet but we are not told that she's an obnoxious self-centred brat who could whine for Britain! It's all about image management. A few years ago I would have used the phrase "impression management" to mean the way we all carefully manage information about ourselves so that we appear in the best possible light. But now that we are all the "star" of our own page, we all have an "image" to manage.

Not that all this is entirely bad. I'm not saying you should never go on a social networking site. But I think a degree of caution is helpful. I look at it as merely an extension of the Christmas card list – that is, the kind of information I would post publicly is of a level that might go in my Christmas newsletter (and we all know how potentially irritating *those* can be). But I'm happy to stay in touch even in this minimal kind of way with a large number of friends, past and present, and occasionally the connections are very significant and helpful.

This might sound ageist, but I can't help feeling that my generation takes all this online social networking with a pinch of salt. It's all very well having lots of "friends" linked to our page, but we know that our close friends are the ones who know our weaknesses and fears, who know the type of information you'd never want posted up publicly. Friends like these only come along now and again. It's over-ambitious to expect to ever have any more than a handful of these treasured people, no matter how many others you also get along with very well.

I'm not sure if the generation who have grown up relating electronically will be able to make this differentiation. Nor do I think they apply the same "filtering" skill that I employ: personal, inappropriate, self-destructive thoughts seem to be out there for anyone to see or comment about. I worry about how real it is to have 300 "friends" on a network site or 900 people who follow you on Twitter. Surely there is a risk of becoming a "persona" rather than a person? Perhaps I'm just fearful of the unfamiliar. But I do think something fundamental is changing about the way we relate to each other. A study into all this by Lady Greenfield, an Oxford professor, reported that these sites can provide "a constant reassurance – that you are listened to, recognised and important".[8] But it's an unreliable and risky source of feedback. How would you feel if you posted up something personal like "I'm feeling down today" and no one responded? These sites also distance us from the stress of face-to-face, real-life conversations, which are "far more perilous and occur in real time with no opportunity to think up clever or witty responses."[9] In other words, our ability to communicate with real people face to face is being seriously hampered.

One young person in this study was quoted as saying that the fact that "you can't see or hear other people makes it easier to reveal yourself in a way that you might not be comfortable with. You become less conscious of the individuals involved, less inhibited, less embarrassed and less concerned about how you will be evaluated."[10] I don't know about you, but embarrassment and inhibition perform a usefully protective function in my life! They have stopped me doing all sorts of things I almost certainly would have regretted.

The other thing that these sites do is allow us to compare ourselves with everyone else. We have far more information than ever before about everything else that everyone else is busy doing, and that in itself poses a challenge. Are we content with who we are and what we do? How do we react when someone else seems to be achieving more or experiencing more than we are? Do we feel ourselves to be under pressure to be busier than we actually are?

There are only twenty-four hours in a day. Once you have done the basics like eating and sleeping, what other "worthy" tasks might you feel ought to be on your list of things to do? You might want to:

- Listen to a news report.
- Take an omega 3/probiotic/vitamin tablet.
- Jog for thirty minutes in the fresh air.
- Clean the dog's teeth.
- Feed the dog.
- Walk the dog.
- Worm the dog (you'll save a lot of time without a dog!)
- Clean your own teeth.
- Floss.
- Moisturize your skin.
- Tidy your eyebrows.
- Read a life-improving book.
- Practise spellings with your child.

- Hear your child or children read.
- Take your child or children to the library.
- Arrange sleepover/birthday party for the kids.
- Make cake for school fair.
- Make an outfit for school play.
- Administer your child's medication/inhaler/ointment/headlice treatment.
- Clean out hamster/guinea pig/rabbit or spend longer amount of time nagging your child to do same.
- Take your child to piano/Brownies/swimming.
- Remember to eat your "five a day".
- Water the plants.
- Sort out stuff for recycling.
- Send a protest postcard on behalf of the oppressed.
- Sign an online petition.
- Read a newspaper.
- Do the ironing.
- Clean the bathrooms.
- Supervise homework.
- Phone a friend.
- Remember to have sex with your partner/husband.
- Revamp your wardrobe.
- Remember to phone your mother.
- Complete assignment for Open University degree/evening class/ distance learning project.
- Open emails and reply.
- Post up status on Facebook – remembering to sound witty and creative.
- Stretch, especially after working on computer.
- Reply to school letters.
- Research wheat-free diet/low-fat diet/low-carb diet as cure for IBS/ big butt/bloated tummy.
- See the latest film.
- Make cake/meal for poorly friend/relative.
- Do shopping for elderly neighbour.
- Meditate/pray/read Bible/keep journal/think uplifting thoughts.

- Cook a healthy and cheap meal for your family (preferably in less time than it takes to read emails).
- Find missing earring.
- Have people in for tea.
- Do brain-training exercise on your Nintendo or complete a Sudoku.
- Replace pens by the phone with pens that work.
- Research a holiday.
- Book a holiday.
- Daydream about your holiday.
- Be "in the moment".
- Be calm.
- Remember to breathe.

It's not hard to see why we are so busy! And that's without a crisis like a car breakdown or a poorly granny. (Interesting to see how much simpler life becomes without pets or children!) Not everything on this list is essential by any means, but I've tried to give a flavour of the things that can oppress us by making us feel that we *ought* to be doing them. Each activity might be worthwhile in its own right but no one can manage all of them. Anyway, apparently not many of us are doing this kind of stuff, even if we think we ought to be. The average Briton is actually spending eight hours a day watching TV, using websites or playing computer games.[11] I don't know what the comparable statistics are for other westernized countries, but I wouldn't be surprised if they were similar. It used to be that eight hours was the benchmark for our working day. Can it really be true that we spend the same amount of time hunched over our computers or slouched in front of our TV screens?

Whatever it is that is taking up our time, we seem to live in a culture that makes us feel that we have no time to do anything, that we have to live at a pace we cannot control. We live in a society that pushes us to relentless work or activity. Although we might value simplicity or solitude, the frantic pace of daily life can seem to put these beyond our grasp.

So far all I've given you is the bad news: all the pressures that you, your daughters, sisters and friends feel all the time to be beautiful, be famous, be successful and be busy. Before we move on, I want to offer you some alternatives, some antidotes, if you like, to the current madness – ways of being that might protect you from living under the pressure of these four big lies dictated to us by culture and society.

I think it's important before we get into the more practical specifics of diet, exercise and self-presentation in detail, that I offer you these four alternative aspirations. These attitudes are more fundamental than learning how to control your appetite. At first glance they might not appear to be as useful as knowing what types of clothes suit you, but adopting these four aspirations could do more for changing the way you live than any amount of surface rearrangement.

The four pressures we've looked at are:

- Be Beautiful.
- Be Famous.
- Be Busy.
- Be Successful.

The four antidote attitudes I'd like to recommend are:

- Be Beautiful (but for different reasons).
- Be Content.
- Be Still.
- Be the Best You Can Be.

It may surprise you that I haven't changed "Be Beautiful". It's a pressure but it's also possible for it to be a positive attitude. It all depends on your motives. I haven't changed it because the opposite, "be ugly" or "don't give a minute's thought to how you look", would not only be unrealistic, it would actually be unhelpful. I have come to believe that the desire to be beautiful is a desire God planted intentionally in the heart of a woman. When Jesus asked us to "consider the lilies of the field" more splendid than royalty in all their glory, he was holding up beauty as an intrinsically good thing. Being able to appreciate beauty, whether it's in a face, a sunset or an array of colours, is something that sets us apart from animals. There will be more on this in a later chapter, but for now let me say that I believe wholeheartedly that God approves of beauty.

However, we need to think about what motivates us to be beautiful. According to Oliver James, there are two main motivators when it comes to looking good: we either want to be more appealing to the opposite sex, or we are using our attractiveness to compete with other women.[12]

Sometimes we do not simply want to appeal to the opposite sex; sometimes we are using our attractiveness to actually manipulate men. We might be sending out a message about our sexual availability or we might dress to make a power statement about who we are. In either case, it's the message that is motivating us to look good. As for competing with other women, any woman knows that if you go to a party it's the other women who will remember what you were wearing. We might want to give out any number of messages through what we are wearing: "I'm young", "I'm fit", "I'm in control", "I'm fashionable" or even negative messages such as "Don't look at me". It has been said that men dress to give only one of two messages: "I'm powerful" (so a sharp suit means "Don't mess with me") or "I'm safe" ("Look, I'm wearing a soft cuddly jumper"). While I do agree that men in general have a far less complex relationship with clothing, they may be capable of more complexity than that!

For his book *Affluenza* the journalist Oliver James interviewed 240 well-off individuals in seven different countries, quizzing them about their values and their state of mind. He draws the interesting conclusion to which I have already referred, that there is a link between the things we value – money, possessions, appearances (both social and physical) and fame – and our level of emotional distress. The more value we place on these four things, the more likely we are to become depressed, anxious or develop addictive behaviours such as becoming a shopaholic, an alcoholic or using other substances to relieve our distress. He is not writing from a Christian perspective, although he notes frequently how having a faith (of any variety) was a significant factor protecting individuals against the effect of warped values. The women he interviewed in Russia and Denmark particularly struck him because they valued the pursuit of beauty for its own sake, for its intrinsic value. They wanted to be beautiful for their own pleasure, because they loved to either make their own clothes, or they enjoyed colour or because self-care was simply a meaningful expression of their own value. It struck him that they were meeting their own criteria of beauty, not competing with other women or trying to attract men. He also noted that those who pursued beauty for its own sake were much less affected by market forces. In other words, they were less affected by the advertising industry intent on making money out of female insecurities, whether by selling expensive cosmetics, clothes with designer labels or slimming products offering effortless weight loss.

It seems to me that this is the ideal way to be. Perhaps now is the time to confess (in case you skipped the preface) that I buy most of my clothes in charity shops or the supermarket. I also moisturize my face with the cheapest moisturizer from the cheapest supermarket. Price is the most important factor when it comes to buying make-up and there are only about seven items in my make-up bag anyway. I wear whatever perfume people gave me for Christmas and the most expensive shoes I've bought in the last year were a pair of specialized shoes for cycling (How sad is that?). My frugality is not all about money, but I simply cannot justify spending a lot on an item of clothing when there are so many better ways I could use that money. So it's partly about ethics, but it's also about fun. I love to find a bargain, I love knowing I've put together an outfit for next to nothing that looks like it's come off a fashion page. After all this confessing, you may now feel that I have totally disqualified myself from writing this book, but believe me, I really like to look good! (Plus the bit about shoes is now out of date, I have recently indulged in an irresistible pair of red leather boots – if a woman's going to mislead you it will be about her age or her shoes!) Looking good helps me feel good, and I enjoy looking good. Being beautiful because it is an expression of who you are, taking care of yourself because you know you have value: these are positive, life-affirming attitudes to have.

The second antidote to the pressures we face is to "be content". Instead of striving to "be famous", be content with who you are. Don't wait to be happy. Don't say *when* I've got my degree, *when* I've landed my dream job, *when* I've made an album, *when* I've made my mark on the world... *then* I'll be happy. The secret of contentment is to be happy now.

Life is what happens today and tomorrow and the day after that. Life doesn't begin once plans, dreams or hopes come to fruition. If we wait to be either famous or fabulous before we allow ourselves to be content, we will have missed a lot of joy along the way. If perhaps you are immune to the pressure to be famous, you may still be holding out for some lesser goal before you allow yourself some joy. Have you ever caught yourself thinking, "Why bother making this house nice –I'd rather live in a bigger one/in a better area" or "I won't buy a nice outfit until I've lost the weight"? Buy the outfit! Decorate the house! Be content with where you are and who you are. Even though in the rest of this book there is going to be a lot of advice about changing your diet, exercise routine and wardrobe, I don't want any changes you choose to make to be born out of discontented self-loathing. Your attitude is everything. Contentment is coming to terms with a less-than-perfect situation that may be at least partly beyond your ability to change. If you can't change a situation, then the only thing you can change is your attitude to that situation. So if you believe you are gorgeous, whatever size you are, that belief will communicate. This point is made brilliantly in a book about relationships by Sarah Litvinoff. Talking about the myth that to be sexy, a woman must be young and beautiful with a perfect body, she says that "it's not the fat that is off-putting, it's the depressed, grumpy, self-loathing female inside the fat that's off-putting".[13] Attitude is everything.

Contented people don't have to prove anything. Discontented people have a constant need to reinforce their achievements or abilities by listing them for you. A discontented person finds it hard to listen well because they are constantly comparing themselves to the person they are trying to get to know. They want to know where they stand in relation to them: are they better off, better educated, better looking? A contented person can listen better than most people because they can accept other people for who they are without their own personal insecurities going off like a set of alarm bells. In short, as Dr J. Sturt says, "people with good self-esteem are comfortable with themselves. They accept themselves, including their short-comings. This acceptance doesn't stop them from making changes; it frees them to do so. They are able to have a balanced estimate of themselves. They can be fully in touch with their emotions but not controlled by them."[14] These are the benefits of contentment, so being content is a worthwhile aspiration.

Contentment is an essential quality, especially when it comes to the ageing process. For many women the pressure to "Be Beautiful" is actually a pressure to stay young. So we have the ridiculous sight of mothers trying to look as young as their daughters and having extreme surgery to ensure they do so. I'm not suggesting you shouldn't take reasonable steps to stave off old age but I am suggesting you should accept the inevitable with a graceful and contented attitude. I have laughter lines because I've laughed a lot. That's a good thing. Not everyone gets the chance to make it to old age, so why should an extra chin come between me and enjoying my grandchildren? At least it doesn't have to be a hairy chin!

"He's blaming his 'extinction' headaches on the poachers but I _know_ it's my fault"

"the grumpy self-loathing female inside the fat" (p.47)

"Be Still" is the best expression I can use for a new attitude to counteract the "Be Busy" attitude. It doesn't quite convey what I mean, because I don't mean to imply that you shouldn't be busy. Some very busy and productive people can still have the quality of being still, and being busy is something most of us can't help. Of course there are ways we can simplify life and activities we could cut out. It's important to recognize when we are simply being busy for the sake of being busy or because we are unwilling to stop being busy. But once we have simplified life as much as possible, the only other choice left to us is to choose the attitude with which we approach our activity. It is possible to be busy with a quiet and "still" attitude of mind. Being still is ruthlessly refusing to be hurried. It's reminding yourself that the world won't end if you arrive a few minutes late, that there is nothing you can do to make the queue move faster, so you may as well accept the slower pace. It's focusing on the task in hand without having half your mind whirring over the next five tasks ahead. When some people tell you they are so busy, it's often simply shorthand for "Listen to me – I'm *so* important!"

People who pride themselves on being busy can sometimes take on more responsibility than is appropriate. I work part-time in a prison chaplaincy, and often there are situations we cannot resolve, or hurts we cannot heal. There is a notice on our office wall that helps us remember our place in the scheme of things: "Please remember that you are not totally, personally, irrevocably, responsible for everything. That's *my* job. Love, God." Busy people can sometimes bustle in and feel an unnecessary responsibility for solving other people's problems. Being on the receiving end of such attention can be very uncomfortable. It's much better to be with someone who is still enough to listen, still enough to simply be with you rather than busying themselves sorting you out. Being still is not an easy attitude to adopt but it's worth cultivating.

"Be the Best You Can Be" is so much more achievable than "Be Successful". You might work really hard at something and never actually "succeed" because of a whole pile of factors beyond your control. But being the best you can be is within your control. The Bible says we should take pride in ourselves without comparing ourselves to others.[15] I love the way that Eugene Peterson renders this idea in his paraphrase *The Message*:

> We will not compare ourselves with each other as if one of us were
> better and another worse. We have far more interesting things to do

with our lives. Each of us is an original… make a careful exploration of who you are and the work you have been given, and then sink yourself into that… each of you must take responsibility for doing the creative best you can with your own life.[16]

Living in a culture that pursues perfection, we have lost sight of the notion that "your best is good enough". After all, if you have done the best that you can, what else could you do? You can let yourself off the hook. You do not carry any blame for the outcome. Being the best that you can be sounds like I am setting a high standard, and I am, but we must not lose sight of the fact that having done our best, we need to allow ourselves the space to "fail". We might be aiming for certain exam grades and not quite make it, or we might have worked for years building up our own business, only to see it crumple due to market forces beyond our control. There is no shame in either of these situations because we have done our best. The word "best" still sounds like a scarily high standard, as in "Sunday best", "best behaviour", "best in the class". Perhaps we need to substitute the phrase "good enough"? For me, the most important area of life where I hope I have done my "best" is being a parent, but I'm so acutely aware of the things that I would like to have done better and regrets over opportunities missed. The fact is, I am not a perfect person, so it's not surprising I have not been a perfect parent. I find it a relief to remind myself that I have probably been a "good enough" parent. I'm not trying to get away with minimal effort, but I am recognizing that there were always factors beyond my control: sleep I didn't get, information I never knew, pressures I couldn't change. So in the circumstances I have been "good enough".

I think sometimes, in relation to our bodies, we need to be able to look in the mirror and say, "Actually, I'm good enough" or "I'm not bad for forty-four [insert your own age]" or "My legs may be short but they are shapely". Given the intensity of feelings generated by the bits of our bodies we dislike, I want you to adopt an attitude that says, "Yes, maybe there are things I can do that will help me be the best I can be", but (and it is a big but) when I have done those things, I need to allow myself the space to say, "I'm good enough". Quite a number of women I've questioned for this book describe exactly this kind of "self-talk" as a way of reaching a place of contentment, which just goes to underline the fact that it's your attitude that matters more than your shape.

Of course, it's all very well me describing these four "antidote attitudes"

– they are easier said than done. How can we be beautiful without looking to see if anyone's noticed? How can we be still and be content in a world which seems to demand constant activity and acquisition? How can we come to terms with our failures and shortcomings if they cause us to feel miserable, self-conscious or envious?

My answer to the "how" question will come in the final two chapters of the book. Before that, the next two chapters will look at two more reasons why we don't feel good naked. If they don't apply to you, you may want to skip ahead to the big three areas of diet, exercise and dress sense. But don't be too quick to rule out the effect of your upbringing and the influence exerted by your religious beliefs – you might just uncover a reality from your past that gives a reason for the way you feel now. Once we've done all we can to be "the best we can be", we will come back to these antidote attitudes and finally learn how to love our bodies and how to love ourselves.

Notes

1. Psalm 139:13; Ephesians 1:4; 2:10; Zephaniah 3:17; Isaiah 1:8; 1 John 1:9; Ephesians 2:10; Psalm 139:16; Matthew 6:32–33.

2. From Oliver James, *Affluenza*, London: Vermilion, 2007, p. 273. The percentage of those working more than 60 hours a week has risen from 10 per cent to 26 per cent since 1998.

3. Ibid.

4. Ibid. "Emotional distress" is a term used by Oliver James, defined as experiencing a mental illness such as depression, anxiety or psychosis in the last twelve months.

5 Ibid.

6. Ibid.

7. Ibid.

8. Report to the House of Lords committee on Internet regulation by Lady Greenfield, professor of synaptic pharmacology at Lincoln College, Oxford, February 2009.

9. Ibid.

10. Ibid.

11. Dr Aric Sigman, a Fellow of the Royal Society of Medicine, writing in the journal *Biologist*, quoted by Martin Beckford, *Daily Telegraph*, February 2009.

12. Oliver James, *Affluenza*.

13. Sarah Litvinoff, *Sex in Loving Relationships*, London: Relate, 2008.

14. Dr J. Sturt, 'Low Self-esteem: untangling the roots', *Care and Counsellor*, Vol. 3, Spring 1993.

15. Galatians 6:4.

16. Galatians 5:26; 6:4 from *The Message Remix*, Colorado: NavPress, 2003.

Chapter 3

If It's Not One Thing, It's Your Mother!

The more I talk to women about their bodies, the more convinced I am that they are exceptionally good at knowing *how* they feel about their appearance but incredibly bad at understanding *why* they feel that way. Ask them to name the feelings generated by a despised physical feature and they will wax eloquent: misery, irritation, frustration, upset, embarrassment, guilt, wistful feelings, self-consciousness, abhorrence, envy and revulsion. When I ask them what has taught them to feel that way, where did those messages come from, who told them a particular feature was unattractive, I find they generally have little idea.

Those strong feeling words I've listed above were not chosen at random. They were from the first twenty-five responses to a questionnaire I put out on body image. The twenty-five women who supplied those words ranged in age from late teens to mid fifties. They were random in terms of background.

As a group more than half of them had rated themselves above 5 on a scale where 1 indicated they felt very bad and 10 meant they felt fabulous. So this was a small group of women, the majority of whom felt reasonably positive about themselves, and yet they still produced such a powerfully negative list of feelings – the vast majority *hated* some aspect of themselves.

So when I asked the follow-up question, "What makes you think this feature is unattractive?", I was surprised that only five of them hinted at an outside influence. The other twenty just repeated for me in even more gruesome detail why their flabby tummy or their podgy thighs were unattractive by saying things like, "It just is unattractive" or "I can see it in the mirror" and "I know it's not what it's meant to look like". They could describe the problem but couldn't tell me why it was a problem. If they had they grown up on a desert island with no mirrors, no media and no one around to tell them that there was a way they ought to look, then one assumes it would never have occurred to them to worry about the size of their bottom, stomach or thighs!

The fact is, you only feel negative about some feature of yourself because someone has told you that that feature is somehow unacceptable. The fact that only five out of twenty-five women even mentioned outside influences speaks volumes about how unaware we are about why we feel the way we do.

The few who did notice they had been affected by an outside influence mentioned things like unkind remarks verging on bullying, and comments from partners, children, mothers or the media. Faith, aged forty-three, said that her friends and family had always felt able to comment freely about her legs in a negative way, and that's what had made her so aware of them. Helen, also in her forties, felt generally very good about herself but was bothered by her belly, which she described vividly as "a pot stuck on my stomach". Interestingly, though, she remembered that her mother was constantly comparing her own belly to other women's and asking her daughter, "Is my belly as big as hers?" So as a small child, Helen got the message loud and clear: a big belly would be a bad thing.

This chapter is about noticing where the messages came from. How did your upbringing affect how you feel about your body now? The messages you picked up may not have been simply verbal. You grew up with a pile of unspoken messages about what really mattered, attitudes to food and attitudes to exercise. In addition, you have adopted, consciously or unconsciously, habits, behaviours and ways of dealing with strong emotions that all have an impact on the shape you are now and how you feel about that shape.

Some women grew up with very clear verbal messages about their bodies, ranging from the more subtle "Do you really think you should be having seconds?" to the completely unsubtle "Have you stuffed your face with all that chocolate?" or "Move your big butt off the sofa." Siblings can rarely resist making comments on gluttony, laziness or size. Nor do they hold back over big ears, goofy teeth, or in my case, the "family" eyebrows. If your mother (God bless her) thinks you are beautiful, the chances are your siblings will correct that view!

Or maybe your family simply didn't pass comment, so you never had the benefit of an affirming remark about your appearance. Generally families like to label and categorize people: "You look like just like your mother" or "You take after your Gran". Lovely, if you come from a long line of Miss World contestants; not so great if what they mean is "You're short and over-weight".

We can't get away from the fact that we have a genetic inheritance, but some of us don't know quite where to draw the line between traits we can control and characteristics that control us. Personally, I feel it's a bit of a cop-out to say, "I can't help it, it's in my genes." It lends a sense of hopelessness to our current situation. To say, "My mother was overweight all her life, therefore I will be too" becomes a self-fulfilling prophecy. The fact is, to a large extent your mother was the weight she was due to the food and lifestyle choices she made. You will be whatever weight you are for the same reason. You are not genetically doomed. You *can* make different choices. "You've got a sweet tooth, just like your Gran" can be said affectionately but it can still sound like a prophetic word in a young woman's head if she believes she can never retrain her palate or break her sugar addiction, simply because she takes after Gran.

A friend of mine made me laugh the other day by describing the "family fat" theory proposed by her brother. He maintains that in their family there is a certain amount of fat distributed amongst the female members. His theory was that this amount remains constant regardless of who is actually carrying the fat at the time. So if mum loses weight, one or other sister will gain it. My friend is currently losing weight and, sure enough, her sister is piling it on. Is the theory correct? Of course it isn't, but it's a good example of a fairly extreme type of self-fulfilling prophecy!

Relatives, especially the older ones, can sometimes take dreadful liberties in what they say about body shape and size. I suppose it's an extension of "My, how you've grown", but being told you're "pleasantly plump", you have

" According to our calculations this is yours "

"'family fat' theory" (p.55)

really "filled out" or you've got "good child-bearing hips" can leave an indelible anxiety deep in our hearts or minds.

It's not a bad idea to stop and think for a moment about any negative messages you received as a child. You don't need to go digging around in your memory. If they have affected you, the chances are they will float to the surface fairly readily. Ask yourself, "Is there any truth in that statement now?" "How much do I live up to that remark?" You don't have to live under the long shadow of hurtful personal remarks, and sometimes it's simply enough to recognize and challenge them. At other times the struggle to overcome the lies we believed about ourselves in childhood can require a great deal of conversation, prayer and patience. It isn't so much the words that were said but the lack of acceptance they conveyed. If all we received were negative messages from someone particularly close to us, like our father or mother, then it can take a very long time to undo the effect of those messages.

While we are on the subject of powerful words, we need to become aware of the words we casually use ourselves. We are so accustomed to saying things like "I should lose some weight", "These jeans make me look fat" or "I'll need a good work-out tomorrow if I eat all this dessert". And maybe these sound fairly innocuous remarks, but they keep our focus on size and food. Exercise is made to sound not like an activity we do for fun but like a means of controlling an out-of-control body. Such statements might be called "Fat Talk".

An American female fraternity called Tri Delta began a campaign in 2008 called *Stop the Fat Talk*, raising awareness that more than 1 million women in the US suffer from an eating disorder. They felt that a change in conversation could lead to a change in attitude. We do say things like "I've been good: I haven't eaten puddings for a week", but since when did abstinence from a sugary carbohydrate make someone morally perfect? It may not sound very different, but it would be so much more accurate and less emotionally loaded to say, "I'm looking after my health by cutting back on sugary desserts." Similarly with exercise: we speak about it in moral terms such as "I've been really bad, I haven't run all week", rather than simple, positive or factual terms like "When I exercise I feel more energetic" or "I feel sluggish when I haven't had the chance to get out and move".

There is often an emotional message behind what looks like a simple statement: "I'll never get rid of this weight" (failure is inevitable, so why try?); "I really shouldn't have seconds" (I know I'll feel guilty but I can't help myself,

I have no self-control); "I'll have to do a few more sit-ups in the morning" (If I try really hard, maybe I can get the body I want, and then everyone will admire me). These are the kinds of things that you might have heard if you grew up with a mother who constantly dieted but never "succeeded", who couldn't relax around food because it induced guilt or anxiety, and who obsessed about exercise but didn't actually seem to enjoy it. The chances are that your approach to these things will feel equally emotionally loaded.

I'd like to suggest that we need to take the emotion out of eating and put the fun back in, but that is easier said than done. There is rarely a week without a headline about the dangers of being overweight, the massive cost of obesity to our health service or the horrors of childhood weight gain. In England, apparently over two thirds of adults and one third of children are obese.[1] We British are the "fattest" people in Europe, not a ratings table we really want to be leading. All of these headlines, combined with Government campaigns to make us all eat less and exercise more, leave a lot of overweight individuals like Jane feeling "uncomfortable, ashamed and second-class to those with perfect BMIs". Jane is size 18–20 and feels like she lives in the middle of witch-hunt around the issue of weight.

In view of all this anxiety, it's hardly surprising that eating has become an emotionally loaded experience. We all grew up with habits and eating patterns that we now know to be bad for us: snacking between meals, eating in front of the TV, rewarding ourselves with something sweet for any "good behaviour", believing we had to eat everything on our plates. Now, as adults, we find ourselves knowing we need to change these habits, sometimes feeling powerless to do so, and then having that failure compounded by a shedload of guilt.

This is a horrible situation to be in. Part of me wants to say, "Enjoy life, enjoy food, stop worrying about your weight", and another part of me wants to say, "Take responsibility – you don't have to live with these habits or messages from your childhood." The reality is that some days (holidays and celebrations) it's absolutely right to say the former, but on almost every other day most of us need to say the latter.

Here are three questions that might help you find out how your upbringing affected how you feel about your body now:

1. What you do remember about how your mother felt about her own body?

Maybe your mother was someone who obsessed about how she looked or, at the other extreme, maybe she was completely indifferent to looking good and a total embarrassment to you at parents' evenings? If she was embarrassed or anxious about her size, you can bet your life you picked up that sense of unease or distress and learnt something along the lines of "Fat people need to fade into the background." It doesn't really matter what size she actually was; the thing that communicated to you was how she felt about being that size and whether she felt good about herself. Whether she was big or small, if she felt good about her size, the chances are you will also feel good about yourself.

When I was about six I wrote a description of my mother in my daily "news" book at school. On parents' evening the teacher left my book open for all the parents to enjoy and my mother discovered herself summarized in three childlike sentences, complete with a picture: "My mummy is short. She is fat. She is happy." Actually, only two of those facts were accurate. I don't think my mother was fat at all. I remember her being fit and active. She played tennis regularly, and she was constantly on the go. I honestly have no idea what size she was, but the fact that she was happy was a far more powerful influence.

2. How did your mother feel about your body?

This might be a harder question to answer because it's possible that nothing was ever said. You might have to surmise how she felt by the way you were dressed. Were you always expected to be well turned out? Did you have constant battles over tomboy jeans or girly skirts? Did she worry over imperfections? How did she like your hair to be cut? What kinds of things were said when you began to choose your own look as a teenager?

Not every little anxiety will stick. I remember on one occasion mum was very anxious about taking me to the dentist. My milk teeth were grey due to a drug she'd had to take whilst pregnant with me. She felt guilty about my appearance but I just remember thinking it was really odd that mum was worried about my teeth. Thankfully, I couldn't care less what my teeth looked like and the adult ones came through the right colour. Now, as a mother myself, I understand her anxiety. I realize that a sense of guilt, sometimes completely unjustified, is always at my elbow. Whatever challenge my children face, I wonder if there is some way I could be held to blame. I am blamed for passing on the family eyebrows – not an earth-shattering fault, but what if my children turned out to be obese? Or suffered from a life-limiting illness? Would that be my fault? But if I go round beating myself up as a mother, I need to remind myself that it is those very same children who will be very deeply affected if they are brought up by a mother who loathes her own body or passes on all her body/food insecurities and anxieties. So we have to try not to let our guilt or anxiety get in the way of expressing acceptance and love for our kids. When we beat ourselves up as mothers and find fault in our kids, we need to remember that they are basing their views of themselves on our views of them. Your mother is the first mirror in which you see yourself.

One of the other factors that informs how we feel about our physical selves is how often and how lovingly we were touched as children. Being hugged, held, appropriately stroked or cherished in some physical way gave us an important subconscious message about our acceptability as a physical person. And the converse is equally true. Your body image is built partly on the verbal and partly on the non-verbal messages you received about yourself.

Reflecting on how your mother or parents felt about your body is not meant to be an exercise in blame. There's really nothing to be gained from saying, "I am the way I am and it's their fault." If the messages have been particularly harsh, you have to come to terms with that and, if possible, forgive them for their shortcomings. But what you cannot do is abdicate your own responsibility to believe better messages about yourself now. Rather than lay blame at anyone's door, it is simply a huge help to understand where the messages we've believed about our bodies have come from and why we feel the way we do. With this information we are better equipped to move forward.

3. What happened to your body in puberty that embarrassed you?

This might seem an odd kind of question,[2] but puberty was probably when you first became truly aware of your own body and, most likely, it would have felt like it was out of control. For boys, suddenly your limbs are too long for your body and you become clumsy; you have the voice of a child one moment and drop an octave the next; and to cap it all, your inner thoughts and feelings might suddenly find expression in your private parts. For girls, particularly those who entered puberty relatively early, there may have been the uncomfortable feeling of having a woman's body with a child's emotions and outlook. Having large breasts at just thirteen might have made you look physically mature, but the emotional maturity to handle unwanted male attention may not have come along till a lot later. You might have been excited about all the changes your body went through during puberty, as signs of growing up and becoming an adult, or you might have felt daunted. How you felt largely depended on how your parents viewed the experience; if your mum lamented your loss of childhood, you might have focused more on what you were losing than on what you were gaining. Maybe your dad suddenly became uncomfortable with you as your body became more feminine. Maybe he became over-protective, worried about your sexual vulnerability ("Cover yourself up, girl!"), or maybe he was possessive, controlling or, in the worst case, predatory. The messages from your father were a key way in which you gauged whether you were physically acceptable and attractive.

If you got the message from either parent that you or your body were unacceptable, offensive or an embarrassment, then you were very likely to grow up feeling a sense of self-hatred and disgust. The extent to which you feel this way might be directly related to the seriousness of their rejection or abuse of you.

The final thing to think about in terms of influence is something less specific than a message but no less influential. The family you grew up in had a "style", a way of relating to each other, a way of responding to problems, a way of handling conflict. By "style" I don't mean anything you could see. I mean a preferred way of behaving that resulted in a particular emotional atmosphere.

If you were brought up in a Christian home the most likely "style" of family life would have been what psychologists call "conflict avoidant". In conflict-avoidant families you are not allowed to be either very happy or very miserable. It is expected that you will stay somewhere near to emotional neutral. Too happy and you might be "counting your chickens before they hatch" – in other words, "too cocky". Too miserable and you were reminded (unhelpfully) that there was always someone worse off than you, so what right did you have to be fed up? The following chapter will look a bit more closely at the effect of religious belief on body image, but I think Christian families are most likely to become conflict-avoidant families because of the huge temptation to give the appearance of "happy families" where all is peace and harmony, children don't swear at their parents, parents don't have rows and emotional scenes are unlikely.

The effect for children brought up in conflict-avoidant families is that they learn to express only a limited range of emotions. If emotions were a rainbow, they do not allow themselves to express the very darkest ones, and one unexpected consequence of this is that they also find it hard to recognize or express the brightest feeling. They live in a kind of emotional neutral. They might look very stable – well adjusted, even – but not being allowed to express the very bad feelings doesn't mean they don't experience them. And if they can't express sadness, anger, misery or despair safely, then they will find unsafe or self-destructive ways to deal with those feelings that are locked away inside. And such self-comfort can often be linked to over-eating, alcohol abuse or self-harm.

If you think you might have come from a conflict-avoidant family, think back to the last time you were aware of feeling bad about something. How did you react? Did you pick up the biscuit tin or the phone? If someone gave you the chance to talk about your problem, did you find you just didn't have the words to express how you felt? Or maybe you felt your feelings were not worth discussing? Maybe you clammed up because you were afraid of making people feel uncomfortable? All of these responses would suggest you have been brought up to clamp down on negative feelings, you don't want to make a fuss, you don't even have the right vocabulary, or you feel terrified about where those negative feelings might take you.

Conflict-avoidant families are families where, if issues even make it out into the open, they are rarely resolved. Nobody rows but negative feelings are just swallowed down. Helena Wilkinson describes them as "shame based families, where it is very important that members look and act appropriately".[3] Sound like any family you know?

If you think you grew up in that kind of a family, you need to allow yourself to broaden your emotional spectrum. It's OK to feel really bad and say so. Your feelings do matter. Maybe you're realizing that you've created that kind of family for yourself. Recognize the problem and give yourself and your children the freedom to express bad feelings. Don't be in too much of a hurry to "tidy away" messy feelings. Be aware if you are using food as a distraction (e.g. "Have a cake, you'll feel better tomorrow"). Maybe you even need to role model if necessary. For example, "Does anyone else round here feel so frustrated they could scream?", "I feel upset if no one seems to be listening to me.", "Sometimes I feel overwhelmed by the bad stuff that happens in the world."

When I was growing up, you didn't express despair because that would mean you weren't trusting God; nor did you get too happy because that would be "counting your chickens before they hatched". This is not actually a proverb found in the Bible, but nevertheless overconfidence was seen as unhelpful. In a conflict-avoidant family lavish compliments might make you big-headed, so you don't get those, and when you mess up you're more likely to get a raised eyebrow rather than a rollicking. On the surface it looks like everyone is very calm and self-controlled but under the surface there may be resentment which will eventually lead to a sense of isolation.

The other main styles for families are "high-achieving" and "chaotic". If you grew up in a high-achieving family you felt valued more for your successes than your personal qualities. Results mattered more than effort. It's likely your parents are highly self-disciplined individuals, fairly driven and used to being in control of their lives. These kinds of parents can produce children who can be very hard on themselves, never feeling like they quite measure up. And this feeling can express itself in less obvious ways: a girl struggling to get high grades at school may find consolation in "controlling her appetite" to the extent that she stops eating. A slim and good-looking young man I met a while ago told me that he felt ashamed of his body in a way that prevented him from joining in with family activities. His story moved me deeply. The more we talked, the more obvious it became that he felt he didn't "measure up" in success terms, to either his father or his siblings. Having nowhere to go with these feelings, he'd made his body the focus. The problem really wasn't his body; he was "fit" in every sense of the word! The problem was his sense of not being "good enough". I still pray for him that he might find the acceptance he craves.

Chaotic families are those where a death, an addiction, a crisis or maybe all these things together leave the adults in the family unable to cope. These adults may lean on their children and the children become "copers". The children then come to look out for themselves because no one else does. They may appear to do fine, to have come out of their chaotic upbringing more mature and resilient, but the risk is that they are so used to pushing aside their own needs, feelings or pressures that they never face up to them. These feelings don't cease to exist; they just bury themselves and turn up again in anger or depression. They don't know how to handle bad feelings constructively because they never had that role modelled for them. Instead they may fall into self-destructive ways of dealing with bad feelings, abusing food, alcohol and their own bodies.

We've talked about some "heavy" stuff in this chapter. How you see yourself, the feelings you have about your body: these things did not just download into your head from outer space! The source of these feelings is easy enough to trace if we are willing to stop and reflect. Sometimes we believe we are unacceptable because we are comparing ourselves to the impossibly high standards of the air-brushed supermodels, but more often the discomfort we feel about our bodies has a much more local source. Working out why you feel the way you do, challenging the messages or even "lies" you were told, moving on from the box into which you were categorized, might all be really important next steps in your quest for self-acceptance, your desire to "feel good naked".

Notes

1. Rebecca Smith, Medical Editor, *Daily Telegraph*, 21 April 2009.
2. These questions are loosely based on ideas from Strober and Schneider, *Just a little Too Thin*, USA: De Capo Press, 2006.
3. Helena Wilkinson, *Beyond Chaotic Eating*, Grand Rapids: Zondervan, 1993.

Chapter 4

Would God Approve?

If you took all the women in your workplace, church or family and put them in a line with those who obsessed most about their appearance at the head of the queue and the least bothered at the other end, where would you put yourself?

All of us know that to be totally, obsessively consumed with anxiety about our appearance can't be a good thing and maybe we know someone we would put in that category. Maybe this woman spends more on her nails each week than we would on the weekly shop. Maybe she has beauty therapy treatments we would consider self-indulgent. Maybe she simply looks better than we do. For whatever reason, we judge her, rightly or wrongly, as *too* concerned about her appearance and we'd rather stand behind her in the line. At the other end of the scale we all know women who seem completely unconcerned about their appearance. This woman may be happily unaware she is a style disaster and we smile at her behind her back. Or maybe her lack of self-care is shouting about her inner pain and we feel either shocked or embarrassed. Either way, we've made a judgment and prefer to think that we'd be standing ahead of her in the line.

We know, as Christians, that we shouldn't really be at one extreme end of the line or the other, but the tricky bit is to know where to stand.

Most of us shuffle into the middle ground, believing that we shouldn't be too showy or ostentatious but we should all at least "make an effort", but none of us agreeing on exactly what would be "too showy" or "too much of an effort". For what it's worth, my opinion is that most Christian women play it safe, rarely making the best of their physical features. We are all too scared to look showy, be misunderstood or seem shallow.

As we have already seen, the media blasts out the constant message that a woman's worth lies in her attractiveness. We've already looked at the huge pressures we are under to be perfect, successful and famous. For a woman who has embraced Christian belief and values, there is a huge opposite pressure to debunk this attitude. My value is not related to my attractiveness. Any hint that it might be makes me want to rebel and demand that I be accepted wearing the fashion equivalent of a brown paper bag. I know there is more to me than appearance. I know I have talents, passions, preferences and creativity but I am a torn woman. A part of me is saying, "Don't judge me for what I look like" and another part is wondering what to wear to a party at the weekend.

Does wanting to look good make me a shallow human being? Am I worrying too much about my appearance? Not enough? Or do I spend almost as much time feeling guilty for all the time I spend worrying about my appearance?

I guess the question "Does God approve?" sums up the Christian woman's ambivalence in this area. Someone completely outside of Christian culture might reasonably ask *why* we would we think that God didn't approve of looking good. The answer to that question lies in three areas: the cultural climate in which we live (or in which we were brought up), the way we interpret some passages from the Bible and, even though we might be unaware of it, the pervasive effect of history.

Your cultural climate

None of us are immune to the way people dress, in whatever community we consider ourselves part of. For the Christian, how people dress in church might be part of what makes up your "cultural climate". Where I go to church no one bats an eyelid if you turn up in jeans and a T-shirt. In fact, if you were to turn up looking dressy, people would probably wonder why. We have abandoned the concept of wearing your "Sunday best", but the wider culture hasn't lost the notion that you should dress up to go to church, so usually it's not hard to distinguish the baptism group from the regulars – they will be much more smartly dressed.

Casual clothes for church are just a reflection of our current culture. Other cultures have a different approach. Recently I had the opportunity to worship in a church in the Caribbean. My husband and son were with me and thankfully they had donned long trousers for the occasion, but they were still the only two men *not* wearing suits and ties. Even the little boys were in suits. All the women and girls wore beautiful dresses, complete with high heels, lots of bling and chiffon. I felt quite plain in my simple black-and-white dress and safe Marks and Spencer sandals. The experience took me right back to my childhood when dressing up for church had been the norm. I grew up in a small nonconformist church that had recently changed from being a Brethren assembly to being a "free evangelical" church. Apart from a John Grisham book title (completely unrelated), you may never have heard of the Brethren. They were a strong movement at the turn of last century. They prided themselves on being biblical and believed that their style of worship was as close as possible to that of the early church. They had a lot of things going for them but fashion sense wasn't one. Female heads had to be covered (hats or scarves), pierced ears were out and long hair was in (on your legs as well as your head).

It wasn't the kind of place that encouraged looking good. At the age of nineteen, after a fair degree of soul searching and Bible study (yes, really!), I rebelled and had my ears pierced. As far as rebellions go, I'm aware that it sounds unbelievably trivial now, but I had been brought up to believe that as my body was the temple of the Holy Spirit, I had no business tampering with it. Pierced ears were more like self-mutilation than self-expression. Improving on your natural looks might make you appear flirtatious, and why would you want to look attractive anyway? What motive could you possibly have for shaving your legs or plucking your eyebrows? Seduction seemed far more likely than the straightforward desire to look less like a gorilla!

None of this was taught, of course. The layout of the temple in Jerusalem was taught in great detail but how to look good in a skirt, I had to work out for myself. Thankfully this culture never flattened my mother's *joie de vivre* for

"Don't stare dear, he's from when they had to make things long enough to grow into"

"Baptism party much more smartly dressed." (p. 69)

colour, style and fashion, and this helped a bit. But at church, demure dress was simply an assumption – demure to the point of frumpy, because some Christians did seem to believe that (in Mike Starkey's words) "dowdiness is next to Godliness, flashy dress is sub-Christian and the height of your sole reflects the state of your soul".[1]

I wasn't alone in this experience. Recently I met a friend in her sixties and complimented her on her outfit. She commented that she now looks twenty years younger than she looked twenty years ago because at that time she was part of a church fellowship that required women to wear long skirts and baggy smocks lest any suggestion of the female form inspire lust!

Thankfully things have improved a lot in recent years. Christians are still a long way off being style icons, but there is a much broader acceptance of fashion as a form of self-expression. However, it still may be helpful for you to reflect on the unspoken assumptions of whatever Christian group, church or community that you belong to. What is it about dress and appearance that is assumed rather than explicitly taught? Is there a pressure to conform? An expectation of how you should dress? And how much are you affected by all these expectations?

What does the Bible actually say?

A good deal of our ambivalence about wanting to look good probably springs from a misguided idea that the Bible would tell us that there are far more important "spiritual" things we should be concerned about. Surely it's at the very least frivolous and possibly even unethical to be concerned about our appearance when half the world starves? Shouldn't we be spreading the gospel, fighting oppression, restoring justice, feeding the hungry or housing the homeless? The world is so full of so many desperate causes, fixing your make-up and styling your hair doesn't seem to rate very highly on a global scale of priorities.

Putting it that starkly does indeed make "self-presentation" sound more like "self-absorption", but the fact is we are not being asked to make a choice. No one is saying you can only do one thing *or* the other. Why not do both? Save the world and look good while you're at it! Heidi Baker has been mightily used by God to save thousands of orphans in Mozambique. So many things struck me about her when I heard her speak: her humility, the intimacy of her relationship with God and her intelligence. But I also noticed that here was a beautiful woman who dressed joyfully and attractively, looked stunning and seemed very at home in her skin. It really made me smile that when God went looking for someone to work among orphans in a Muslim country, he didn't send a serious-looking man – instead his eyes fell on a "blonde bombshell"!

Several passages of the Bible are quoted and misunderstood more than others. In Matthew 5, for example, we are told that we ought not to worry about what to wear, and the implication is sometimes drawn that this shallow pursuit is the reserve of the ungodly, "for the pagans run after all these things" (Matthew 5:32). In fact, what Jesus is talking about is the difference between trust and anxiety. He is not lecturing on the evils of fashion. He is not downgrading beauty. Quite the opposite. By pointing to "the lilies of the field" he is suggesting that to be beautiful or attractive is a very good thing.

Then there are two other passages that appear to confine women to dull "decency" and bargain-basement apparel. Paul writes in 1 Timothy 2:9–10: "I also want women to dress modestly, with decency and propriety, not with braided hair or gold or pearls or expensive clothes but with good deeds, appropriate for women who profess to worship God." Then in 1 Peter 3:3–4 Peter writes to wives that "your beauty should not come from outward adornment, such as braided hair and the wearing of gold jewellery and fine clothes. Instead it should be that of your inner self, the unfading beauty of a gentle and quiet spirit, which is of great worth in God's sight."

At first sight it seems hard to argue against these passages. But we need to remember that these instructions were written to particular people in a particular place who lived in a particular culture and in answer to a particular problem. If we shared all those particular experiences with the original readers, then the particular advice might well apply, but given that we don't, we have to look at the passage and ask ourselves, "What did this mean to them at that time?" and then "What principles can we take from it that apply to us now?"

There is good evidence to show that at that time women who "dressed up" in public were announcing sexual availability and a desire to be unfaithful wives. Hair braiding was considered sexually attractive and a woman's hair was considered so powerfully provocative that wearing it uncovered, let alone braided and adorned, was the ancient equivalent of a see-through blouse and a bum-scraper dress. Paul is teaching here about immodesty and sexual morals, he is not condemning looking good *per se*. Likewise, Peter is talking about the source of beauty. He is not saying you should aim to be ugly. He is not saying anything about whether you should or shouldn't be attractive. He's simply saying that the source of beauty is deeper than surface rearrangements.

These two passages seem to be the only ones in the whole Bible which refer directly to women and clothes, and because of this they have assumed an inappropriate status. But they should not be read on their own. They have to be read in context, along with everything else the Bible has to say about clothes. And the Bible has a lot to say about clothes. If you remember the opening story in Genesis, it was God who made the first clothes to cover the shame of Adam and Eve who had realized their nakedness following the fall. Again, a lot of people interpret this very negatively, that clothes are some kind of functional necessity, a part of the fallen world, only necessary because we had sinned. If this were the case, now that we are redeemed, why aren't we all walking round naked?

Look below the surface of the story and you can see that God's provision of clothes is actually the first step in the process of restoring humankind's dignity and honour. Adam and Eve were not just clothed in as functional a way as possible to keep them warm; they were "robed for office", and over and over again in the Bible, clothing is a "constant and pervasive symbol of dignity and authority".[2] Nakedness is almost always a symbol of shame, reserved for the destitute, the conquered or the deranged. Unfaithful Babylon is described as removing her veil, lifting her skirts and baring her legs, an example of clothing being used symbolically to depict depravity.[3] A passage in Ezekiel reverses that image gloriously. God is describing, in the form of a parable, how he rescued his people Israel and restored them from slavery:

> I clothed you with an embroidered dress and put leather sandals on
> you. I dressed you in fine linen and covered you with costly garments.
> I adorned you with jewellery; I put bracelets on your arms and a
> necklace around your neck and I put a ring on your nose, ear-rings on
> your ears and a beautiful crown on your head. So you were adorned
> with gold and silver; your clothes were of fine linen and costly fabric
> and embroidered cloth.[4]

This is a God who loves quality and beauty, not a God who is into functional polyester!

And Jesus told a story about the Prodigal Son – how he came back in rags and tatters and the father rushed to greet him, putting his best gown round his shoulders and a ring on his finger. Rich clothing symbolized the dignity of a son. He was not a hired servant, he was the returning son. Clothing in the Bible is often a demonstration of one's inner state and a sign of honour; hence the ornate way in which priests were clothed. Conversely, deep grief was expressed by tearing one's clothes; the distressed look was meant to give expression to a distressed heart. The demon-possessed man, once he has been freed by Jesus, is found sitting at Jesus' feet "dressed and in his right mind".[5]

Paul even uses clothing as an image of redemption itself, of the way we should change when we become Christians. He says we "clothe ourselves with Christ" (Galatians 3:27) – and what would this look like? We would "clothe ourselves with compassion, kindness, humility, gentleness and patience" (Colossians 3:12). OK, he's not saying "clothe yourselves with Armani, Gucci and Oscar de La Renta", but he is using the idea of clothing in a wholly positive way, implying that clothing should be a positive and legitimate expression of who we are.

The women in the church that Peter wrote to might well have worn fine linen and jewellery. The key point Peter wanted them to know was that they should not root their entire sense of self-confidence in them. As Mike Starkey says, the Christian woman's "public image must never become a substitute for a sense of who she really is".[6] I guess this comes back to what we were saying in Chapter 2 about motives. The women from Russia and Denmark were motivated to look good for their own sakes, not to compete with other women, not to attract men, but simply because self-care and self-presentation was all about self-expression. Our motivation for looking good comes from the sense that we have value. We are loved, we are worth something.

The influence of history

So, given that the overwhelming message of the Bible is that each individual is of great worth to God, how come Christians over the years, particularly in Western cultures, have "dressed to depress"? Our ambivalence about colour, design and adornment has more to do with historical influences than biblical ones. The trouble is, most of us are unaware that the way we think now is dictated by years of thinking that has gone before. We tend to be unaware of the fact that our cultural landscape has been shaped by previous thinkers, philosophers and cultures. We think we are thinking our own thoughts (e.g. "maybe God doesn't approve of looking good"), but actually we have been directed to think that way by influences we probably couldn't even name.

In the film *The Devil Wears Prada* there is a wonderful confrontation that makes this exact point. The central character, a young girl dressed in a blue sweater and a frumpy skirt, is caught laughing at what she sees as the fashion world's obsession with detail. Her boss, a fashion magazine editor played by a fantastically haughty Meryl Streep, turns on her, picking on her blue sweater to explain:

> What you don't know is that sweater is not just blue, it's not turquoise, it's not lapis, it's actually cerulean and you are also blithely unaware of the fact that in 2002 Oscar de La Renta did a collection of cerulean gowns, then I think it was Yves St Laurent who showed cerulean military jackets. Then cerulean quickly showed up in the collections of eight different designers and it filtered down through the department stores and trickled down into some tragic corner where you, no doubt, fished it out of some clearance bin. However, that blue represents millions of dollars and countless jobs and it's sort of comical how you think you've made a choice that exempts you from the fashion industry when in fact you're wearing a sweater that was selected for you by the people in this room, from a pile of "stuff".[7]

Likewise, whether we know about them or not, none of us are immune to the influences in the past that have shaped the present. One of the most powerful of those influences was the Greeks. They had the idea that the body was bad and the soul was good. This simple idea has become the foundation of what we now understand as the sacred/secular divide. This is the idea that there are some things that are sacred or spiritual (prayer, Bible reading, acts of mercy, church attendance, tithing, worship etc.) and other things that are secular and not at all spiritual (eating pizza, watching TV, having sex, putting on make-up, shopping for clothes). Basically everything to do with your body is bad, temporary and shallow, and everything to do with your soul is good, eternal and far more important.

It's this idea, more than anything else, which makes us wonder, when we reach for the hair-straighteners, whether God really does approve of looking good. But this is a Greek idea, not God's idea. It's really important we remember that because many of the New Testament writers were also deeply influenced by this idea, they can even sound at first glance as if they support it. God, however, does not see us as a person with a variety of parts – a soul, a body and a spirit – and even if he did, one part is certainly not less important or more "shameful" than the others. God sees us as a whole. What we wear, how we look and what we eat is all just as interesting to him as how we pray, when we worship and what proportion of our income we give away.

God has always delighted in women. Women were created to be beautiful and not just for functional reasons. Both women and men bear the image of God. In Genesis chapter 1 we are told that "God created human beings in his own image, in the image of God he created them; male and female he created them" (1:27). This idea of being an image bearer is a very important one. It means that we humans somehow represent God to the world. We show what he's like. The image is very blurred because we're far from perfect and only Jesus was the perfect image bearer, but every single human being, male and female, reflects in some way the glory of the God who created them.

One of the problems began in the early years of the church when some church fathers you may never have heard of said that women were not created in the image of God. Only men were. Women were somehow secondary, imperfect, carnal, inferior. Augustine, Aquinas and Calvin (male theologians, not fashion designers!) all expressed negative views about women. Here's what another one of them said regarding what women should wear: "Woman should dress in humble garb, walking about as Eve, mourning and repentant… that she might more fully expiate that which she derives from Eve – the ignominy and odium of human perdition."[8] In other words, living in a fallen world is all Eve's fault, womankind in general should be thoroughly ashamed of themselves and dress accordingly!

Now do you understand why you sometimes wonder if God is ambivalent about women? You have been conditioned to think that way. You also probably think in the way the Greeks have conditioned you to think. Whenever you express a view along the lines of, "It's what inside that counts", you are expressing a view that what's on the outside is somehow superficial or irrelevant. And there's a part of me that agrees with you but another part of me that says don't undervalue beauty. The ability to appreciate beauty is something that sets us apart from animals. God appreciates beauty. There is no actual need for a sunset to be beautiful; you do not see animals gazing in awe at the colours in the sky. God is not a God of functionality. He is a God who loves variety, colour and extravagance. Why else do the oceans teem with multicoloured creatures that just a few people ever get to see? If God was a functional God, surely we could have managed with a few thousand less species of flowers or birds or animals? But creation reflects God's character and what creation tells us is that God loves variety and beauty.

Even modern-day theologians as respected as Richard Foster, who wrote *Celebration of Discipline*, urged people to have clothes that were "practical rather than ornamental".[9] That makes me feel kind of sad, because even the poorest people in the world value ornament and colour. Why should Christians be condemned to be plain and mundane? Expressing who we are by what we wear and how we look says something about our value. I remember reading a moving account from Belsen, a notorious concentration camp. When the Allies went in to free the survivors, naturally they gave out clean clothing, hot food and medicines. But for the women, it was being given a lipstick that somehow restored their hope and sense of themselves as valued people. Even five pairs of sensible shoes would never have had the same effect! We clothe people not just for modesty but for dignity. The God I know isn't a penny-pinching, practical, utilitarian God who despises excess.

Mike Starkey makes an excellent point when he asks "where does the image of God reside?" Is it some "treasure buried deep within us… a deep, hidden aspect of our inner being"?[10] He argues instead that the image of God can be seen in the totality of who we are and what we do. In other words, forget all this inner and outer stuff – you are a whole person and God is interested in every part of you. Getting closer to God is not achieved by being dismissive of your body. He gave you a brilliant body, he wants you to delight in the way it works, in the wonderful things it can do and yes, even in the way it looks.

We know that our culture is often obsessed with designer labels, but God is the ultimate designer and each of us carries his designer label. God has brightened every corner of his world, putting his creativity on display for any who want to see it. Part of our calling is to brighten up the corner of the world where we have been placed, to reflect God's image in who we are, and how we look forms part of that reflection. So "let your little light shine!"

NOTES

1. Mike Starkey, *Fashion and Style*, Crowborough: Monarch, 1995.
2. Ibid.
3. Isaiah 47:2–3.
4. Ezekiel 16:10–13.
5. Mark 5:14.
6. Mike Starkey, *Fashion and Style*.
7. *The Devil Wears Prada*, Twentieth Century Fox, 2006. Directed by David Frankl, loosely based on the book of the same name by Lauren Weisberger.
8. Tertullian, third century AD.
9. Richard J Foster, *Celebration of Discipline*, UK: Hodder & Stoughton, 1980
10. Mike Starkey, *Fashion and Style*.

Chapter 5

Making the Most of Your Body: The "F" Factor

O that this too, too solid flesh would melt.
Shakespeare's *Hamlet*

I'm on two diets: you don't get enough food on one.
Slogan on a fridge magnet

A balanced diet is a burger in both hands.
Quip on a greeting card

Lord, if you can't make me slim, please make my friends fat.
Dieter's prayer

"F" stands for food. It also stands for "Fabulous" and personally, I think food is fabulous. I love to eat. I love lasagne. I love roast beef and Yorkshire puddings with lashings of gravy. I love sticky toffee pudding and lemon meringue pie. I'm not a great cook but I'm a good eater! Whoever wrote the song "Food, Glorious Food" clearly felt the same way.

Unfortunately "F" is not just for "fettuccini", "fudge" and "fries". It also stands for "fat" and for "fear". If, like me, you've ever tried to lose weight, you'll know that food, fat and fear are three ideas that are very closely related in the mind of a dieter. Come to think of it, "F" is also for "failure", and when it came to dieting, I was definitely one of those.

Have you ever met "the successful dieter"? Isn't she irritating? Obsessed about calorific value and portion size, she is annoyingly smug about her slim status and will tell you in detail how much she has lost: pounds, ounces and inches from her waist/thighs/hips. It's always been "so much easier" than she expected; her weight-loss plan is "just so simple" and you can feel the evangelistic fervour in her voice as she suggests that it could work for "even you". "Even *me?*" you think, not knowing whether to feel ashamed or indignant, but either way she's not getting an invite to dinner and possibly not a Christmas card next year either. I really do *not* want to be that person… again.

Because, you see, I am a "successful dieter" as well as a "failed dieter". I was a failed dieter before I became a successful dieter. These days I prefer not to think of myself as a dieter at all. Let's forget dieting – I'm a "healthy eater". In my late thirties I did the whole diet thing, learnt a lot, lost two stones, went a bit obsessive about it for a while, bored the pants off a lot of my friends and was probably even dropped from the odd Christmas card list. Then I had an epiphany. That's not an angelic announcement; it's just a moment when everything becomes clear. I thought to myself "What *have* I done? Have I signed up to this for the rest of my life? Will I *never* be able to eat ice-cream again without feeling guilty? Will I *always* be weighing myself and feel like I'm in a constant state of war with flabbiness?" It was a depressing thought.

I'd been happy to lose the weight, but it felt like food was beginning to lose all the happy associations I'd had with it: fun, friendship and good times together. I didn't want to go to weddings and wonder what I could eat. I didn't want to bake with my kids and *not* lick the bowl (as if that was ever likely!). Mostly I felt an overwhelming dread that I had started something I couldn't

"It's aversion therapy
- this is what a **really** fat version of me looks like!"

"Mostly I felt an overwhelming dread." (p.82)

maintain. When you read all of those "success" stories in diet magazines, no one ever finishes their article by admitting to that kind of fear.

I used to love those "I lost four stone and changed my life forever" stories – they were so motivating. But having met a few of those "stories" who have in real life later returned to their original weight or heavier, I realized that simply being successful once didn't mean you'd beaten your food demons forever. There was no way I could maintain the strict regime that had helped me lose the weight, and I really didn't want to be *that* preoccupied anyway, so it felt like I had a bleak choice between two options: struggle on and stay slim, or let my self-restraint slip and watch the pounds pile back on.

Eight years down the line from that moment, I think I've found that there is a third way, but I'm running ahead of myself. Like all good "dieter stories", I should really go back to the beginning.

As a child I wasn't overweight. I had a sweet tooth but not many opportunities to indulge it. I was a timid eater, not keen to try new things but content with a limited number of favourites. I'd been pretty much the right weight for my size even though I probably downed doughnuts, chocolate-flavoured cereal and sugary snacks with the best of them. Come to think of it, I know I did. One of my aunties used to call me "the 'Mini-Roll Kid'". She'd take great delight in providing platefuls of chocolate-coated mini-rolls every time we went to tea. I probably ate the lot! But when I reached my teens I found I was in that happy period of life when it didn't seem to make any difference what I ate.

I never really worried about my weight till after I'd had my children in my twenties. I had got married at twenty-two. Yes, I still have my dress and I even tried it on again not so long ago. (No, it didn't fit – were you seriously thinking it would? I may have shaped up, but let's not get silly here!) I was probably around a size 12, with boobs that stayed in place, and no other bits of me that sagged or slumped. Oh happy day!

And then I got pregnant.

I rather enjoyed being pregnant because I rarely threw up and thought the whole idea of "eating for two" was pretty neat. Not surprisingly, after each nine-month period of pleasant over-indulgence, there was a satisfyingly "bonny" baby (big babies are never "fat", they are always "bonny" – why *is* that?) and a slighter fatter me. The problem was incremental, so perhaps it's just as well I stopped at two. Breast-feeding is meant to help you lose weight, but I felt I had to be sure I was taking in enough in order to be putting out all that goodness, so my babies got bigger and so did I. (Besides, it's the only time in my life I've had "Dolly Parton" boobs – what a bonus!)

It isn't that I didn't try. As the children began to grow up, I would occasionally attempt to lose weight. The pattern was that having worked myself up into a lather of self-disgust (something along the lines of "My butt is so gross!" or "There are five rolls of fat round my middle!" would usually do the trick), I would announce my intention to my beloved. Annoyingly, he would fail to correct the expressed view of my anatomy and would raise his eyebrows in a "so tell me something I haven't heard before" kind of way. This would make me mad and I'd think, "I'll show him!" And I really did think I would, because in my head I still felt like the skinny teenager – this fat mummy person wasn't the real me. I was really the slim person inside the "fat mummy" suit.

Next, I would sit down and list all the foods that I was *never* going to eat again: biscuits, cakes, anything with pastry, chocolate and so on. Then I'd pick a day and resolve that from that moment onwards none of these forbidden, sinful items would ever cross my lips. I would exercise masterful self-control and lo, the real slim me would suddenly emerge.

It never happened.

Every time I followed this plan, I would actually put weight on, usually about half a stone, pretty quickly too. Then I'd get fed up – "All this self-deprivation and nothing to show for it!" – so I'd give up. And once I'd given up, well, what the heck, "If you're going to have one chocolate biscuit you may as well have two." So the cycle went round full circle: I'd felt fat, I'd tried to tackle it, I'd failed, I was even fatter, so I'd feel worse, and so on.

Dieting became a self-defeating exercise. Looking back, I can see there were several flaws in my plan. Number one: I focused so much on food, it was all I could think about, so I ate more of the stuff that wasn't on my list to make up for the "forbidden" foods. Number two: I labelled a lot of foods as "bad". In fact, there is nothing "good" or "bad" about food. Food is food. It doesn't have intrinsic moral qualities. What's good or bad about it is our ability or inability to eat it responsibly. How many times have you heard a dieter say, "I have to cut chocolate out all together because once I start, I just can't stop"? Is she serious? It conjures up a picture of someone so out of control that she is doomed to eat chocolate for all eternity. (For some of you that may not be too distressing an image!) I know what she *really* means is, "I can't trust myself to exercise control so I have to abstain", but if you never learn to exercise control, how *long* do you have to abstain for – the rest of your life? Will you *never* be able to have chocolate again? Now, that would be a distressing idea!

The third thing I did wrong was to try to exercise self-control without ever addressing the issue of why I was over-eating in the first place. One of the reasons I failed at dieting was that I didn't like being hungry. This sounds so obvious; you're probably thinking, "Is she stupid? Didn't it occur to her that losing weight might just possibly involve being just a teeny bit hungry for at least some of the time?" Well yes, it did occur to me, but I was actually afraid of being hungry, and the day I found out that it was possible for me to feel hungry and yet not actually die was another revelation!

The only thing I can put this fear down to is that in my late teens I occasionally had near black-out experiences. I would suddenly feel really bad, clammy, light-headed and very, very irritable. By trial and error I discovered that a sweet sugary snack like a biscuit or a chocolate bar would resolve all these symptoms immediately. I did ask my doctor about it and he sent me for a test to see if I was diabetic. I wasn't. But he missed the opportunity to explain to me that even though I wasn't diabetic, my problem was still sugar related. I was riding the "sugar rollercoaster" and the near black-outs were simply the moments when the sugar level in my bloodstream dropped suddenly. My remedy, a dose of yet more sugar, worked in the short term but didn't get me off the rollercoaster. It was quite a few years before anyone did eventually explain the sugar rollercoaster to me, and that was another moment of revelation. (If you've never heard of it, I'm going to get round to explaining it later in this chapter.)

Anyway, the result of this experience was a fear of being hungry. I really thought I might faint, become irrational or even die if I didn't eat. And as you can imagine, a determination to avoid being hungry at all costs isn't exactly an asset when it comes to a weight-loss regime.

The final factor that doomed me to failure from the outset was the fact that I didn't have a *good* reason to lose weight. Yes, I was overweight but that wasn't a good enough reason. What I did have was a *bad* reason, in fact a whole bunch of bad reasons. The reason I wanted to lose weight was because I had swallowed whole a huge pile of myths about slim women.

Let me try and put this in a visual way: imagine a tug of war between two women. One is skinny and one is fat. These two women and this tug of war is just a description of what was going on in my head. Some days Skinny Woman tugged and I thought, "I really want to be slim"; then the next day Fat Woman pulled on the rope and I thought, "Why should I have to be slim?"

Skinny Woman's arguments were all statements of "fact". She would say things like, "Slim is sexy", "Slim is attractive", "Slim people are successful", "Slim people have happier lives, relationships, careers". Fat Woman's arguments were all indignant questions: "Why should I have to conform to some media-dictated standard?" "Doesn't *who* I am matter more than how big I am?" "Why not notice me for my intelligence, wit, creativity, compassion?" "Why should I be judged by my dress size?"

Fat Woman was about as grumpy as Slim Woman was seductive. The trouble was, Fat Woman was telling the truth.

By now you've either "got the picture" or you think I'm verging on the edge of a personality disorder. Of course, I know there aren't *really* two women in my head pulling on a rope, but that was how it felt. The reason I was a failed dieter was because Skinny Woman's reasons were all a load of rubbish. If I was ever going to diet successfully, Skinny Woman would have to put on a bit of muscle and provide me with a stronger, more truthful reason to lose weight. Eventually she did.

The reason I finally did succeed at losing weight and the only reason why I continue to be careful over my weight is that Skinny Woman transformed herself into "Healthy Woman".

Meet Healthy Woman. Here are some of the things *she* says when Fat, Flabby Woman pulls on the rope and tempts me to pig out: "Being healthy means I get to live longer", "Being healthy means I get to enjoy life better", "Being healthy means I am less likely to suffer from high blood pressure, diabetes, joint pain, or any number of life-limiting or life-threatening conditions", "Being healthy means I can achieve goals like long-distance bike rides or sponsored walks. I sleep better. I move better, I feel better because my body simply works altogether better when I'm not asking it to carry around a load of excess weight."

I'd found some good reasons at last!

Next I found a good class. There are any number of good ones out there. They all work along the same principles: you're paying for the privilege, someone weighs you every week and there is a sense of solidarity and companionship in the journey. They are almost always a good idea. There is one down side but more of that in a moment.

Losing the weight took me about six months. It was all "much easier than I'd ever imagined" and I did feel a heady sense of self-control. I used to go to a high-street store to weigh myself and kept all the little printouts in my purse. I would take off my coat and my shoes and wasn't beyond taking off my belt if I thought it was too heavy! I got just a little too carried away and lost just a little too much for a while – just enough to understand why anorexics get hooked on the sense of power that comes from seeing pounds fall away.

And then I had that epiphany I told you about at the start of this story. Ever since then I've been learning to find the right balance between Skinny Woman, Fat Woman and Healthy Woman. I've been learning about how to tune into my own appetite, how to make small changes that make big differences, and how to better savour the pleasure of food. And it's those things I want to share with you now.

To diet or not to diet?

Susie Orbach, in her excellent book *Bodies*,[1] points out that "if diets worked, you would only have to do it once". She suggests that diets have a recidivism rate as high as 95 per cent. What that means is that 95 per cent of people who lose weight on a diet will put all that weight back on once they have stopped dieting. Other studies have shown it might be that only a third to two thirds of dieters regained all the weight.[2] Either way, it's a pretty depressing failure rate and enough to put you off the whole idea of dieting. Diet companies rely on this recidivism rate. If we didn't keep "failing" we wouldn't keep coming back to either try again or look for a new magic formula. They would be out of business and publishers wouldn't be churning out all the new diet books that come into our bookstores weekly. The truth is, we are suckers for all this stuff. We think it's our fault, we didn't "follow the plan", we cheated, we gave up, or maybe the diet simply wasn't "the right one" for us. We've tried the cabbage diet, the grapefruit diet, the "no carb" diet and so on. There are even diets based on your blood group!

In the UK it has been estimated that about 25 per cent of adults and 20 per cent of children are obese. The UK government recently announced an intention for every adult to undergo a weight assessment with their doctor.[3] So soon we may be required to stand in line to have our podgy bits poked and a finger waved in our face telling us to "shape up" – not an enticing prospect.

It's partly the fact that so many people are making money out of our fears and insecurities that puts me off dieting. In the US the diet industry was estimated to be worth $100 billion in 2006. In the same year the US department of Education Budget was only $127 billion.[4] That seems slightly mad to me. Are we really getting our priorities right? It also seems obscene that we in the West are fixated on consuming as few calories as possible when the majority of the two-thirds world so badly need every calorie they can lay their hands on.

So dieting makes me uneasy for financial and for ethical reasons. Even if you put those to one side, you still need to answer the question, "Can dieting work?" Could you possibly be one of those (few) people who don't put back on all the weight?

To answer that you need to understand about your metabolic rate. This is the rate that your body uses up calories. Think of it as being rather like the accelerator pedal on a car. Put your foot down and the engine revs go up and you'll use up your fuel much quicker. Ease back on the revs and your fuel will last longer. The fuel is the fat in your body and the accelerator pedal is your metabolic rate.

The trick to losing weight is to burn up more calories than you eat. That's the whole formula. Forget the shelves of books that will tell you otherwise. It really is that simple. Eat less, burn more. It sounds like a recipe for success? Well, it would be if your body didn't play a nasty trick on you as soon as you start to eat less. Not long after reducing your intake and losing some weight, your body panics, assumes that you might have to survive a famine and slows your metabolism down by 15 to 30 per cent. This is why you often feel lethargic on a diet and why, after losing the initial few pounds, you reach a plateau and find it hard to shift some more, even though you are still eating less.

Of course there is a way round this sneaky trick the body plays on you: you have to find ways to keep your metabolism revved. This is mostly down to exercise. The more exercise you do, the more muscle you will have. The bad news is, muscles weigh more than fat, but the good news is, a muscle will burn fat all the time, even while you are sleeping, whereas fat just sits there. Exercise is a good idea for all sorts of reasons other than simply building up muscles to help you lose weight. That's why we'll spend the whole of the next chapter on ways to get moving. For the time being we just need to note that trying to diet without increasing your activity levels is a pretty pointless plan.

There are ways of dieting that do definitely work. I'm a "successful" dieter, so I must have found one, surely? I've already told you that I joined a class and I really enjoyed the whole experience. I learnt a lot about portion size and food values. I was inspired to cook healthy meals from fresh ingredients and my whole approach to food was changed. The camaraderie was great, and the encouragement and accountability side of things definitely worked for me. So I wouldn't put anyone off joining a class and sticking with the programme at least once in your life.

The problem came when I tried to readjust to "normal" life. I realized then what I had just undergone was a hugely performance-based exercise: I was rewarded each week by a new stamp in my card, the warm approval of my class leader ("Another 2 pounds lost – well done, Sheila!") and the envious glares of the somewhat larger ladies in the weekly queue for the scales. No wonder I enjoyed the experience. But I was left wondering if all this "performance" was good for my soul?

Then, once I'd lost the weight and all that positive feedback dropped away, I was on a "maintenance diet" (i.e. maintaining my target weight), but what I seemed to maintain the most was my vigilance and anxiety that all that effort would come to nothing. Would I be a success or a failure?

And that's probably the biggest problem I have with diets: the notion of success and failure. Those words are so loaded with emotion. The fact that you've failed to lose weight doesn't mean you've "failed" as a person. Very closely linked to the idea of "performance" is the issue of "control". Control is another reason why I think diets are generally a bad idea. Control can easily get out of hand and rapidly descend into obsession. I remember one evening while I was on my diet I dropped in to see a friend. While I was there she gave me a glass of squash to drink. At the time my dieting discipline insisted that I write down either the calorie content or the "points" value of everything I ate or drank. I remember feeling very unhappy for an hour or two after because I hadn't been rude enough to ask her if I could read the bottle and work out the calorie content of my drink. And then I came to my senses and the sensible part of my brain told me, "It was a glass of squash – hardly the equivalent of chocolate brownies with ice-cream! It's *not* going to ruin your diet!" I did finally laugh at myself, but the fact that it had upset my emotional equilibrium, albeit temporarily, warned me that I was on the verge of becoming a control freak.

Control is a word we often associate with eating disorders. Usually if someone is going to develop an eating disorder there are other psychological factors that give rise to it, but "going on a diet" is obviously the trigger event. It has been shown that girls who diet are twelve times more likely to binge and develop bingeing as a way of dealing with their food.[5] My experience of diets is that they are more likely to encourage chaotic eating. They also make us afraid of food, which I think is intrinsically unhealthy.

So to answer the question at the head of this section: diet if you must, but remember that recidivism rate of 95 per cent. A diet will work but it will only work in the short term. You do not want to end up feeling like a performing seal (albeit a slim one) or a hamster in a wheel, constantly working hard to go nowhere. Finally, bear in mind that slightly overweight people, with a BMI of between 25 and 29.9, have actually been shown to live longer on average than those with a "normal" BMI of between 18.5 and 24.9.[6] If all that lot hasn't put you off the idea of dieting, by all means go ahead, but I would just ask that you don't do it out of self-loathing. A diet can be a really useful way of reeducating yourself for the long term and also a way to revive your interest in the quality rather than quantity of your food. For these two aspects alone going on a diet can be a helpful exercise. But just as we are reminded that "A dog is not just for Christmas", so a diet should not be for life. There has to be a better way of living that being on a constant diet.

Are you really fat?

I suppose logically this question should have come before the "To Diet or Not to Diet?" question. After all, if you're not fat, why would you want to diet? But as all women know, being actually fat and just feeling fat are not logically connected in the way you might expect. The slimmest of women can still feel fat and the averagely built, but not actually overweight woman can feel herself to be grossly overweight.

So "Am I really fat?" is a subjective question. There are ways of making objective judgments about whether or not you are actually fat (such as body mass index or waist-to-hip ratio), but I understand that in one way these are completely irrelevant to the question of whether you feel fat or not. If you feel "really" fat, your actual size may have nothing to do with these feelings. And the chances are you are more likely to go on a diet on the basis of these subjective feelings than hard factual measurements. In a survey I carried out for this book in which I had about 130 responses, only three women said they were happy with the size they were. All the others wanted to be at least a size smaller than they actually were; this desire to be smaller was consistent regardless of whether they were a size 10 or a size 20.

This is what I mean when I say we are more controlled by subjective feelings than hard data. So it feels self-defeating to even suggest that hard factual measurements do matter – but they *do* matter! They can restore our sense of perspective. They can give us a guide as to what is normal and perfectly OK. Comparing ourselves to a sensible scale might be a wiser move than comparing ourselves with our peers, especially if our friends are like strings of spaghetti. So if you want to try to make an honest assessment, here's how you work out your body mass index and your waist-to-hip ratio.

To calculate your body mass index, divide your weight in kilos by your height in metres squared. For example, if I am 1.6 metres tall and weigh 69 kilos, I will multiply 1.6 by 1.6, which equals 2.56. Then divide the weight by this figure: 69 divided by 2.56 gives a BMI of 26.7. The ranges that are considered normal are 20.1–25 for men and 18.7–23.8 for women.

Your waist-to-hip ratio is becoming widely regarded as a more accurate predictor of health outcomes. For men it should be around 0.9 and for women about 0.85. The higher the number, the greater the risk of diabetes, cardiovascular disorder and, for women, ovarian cancer. It's more accurate because it tells you where you are carrying your fat, and fat carried around your middle is more likely to give you heart problems. You can work out your waist-to-hip ratio by dividing the measurement of your waist by that of your hips.

While you've got your calculator out, let's get one last calculation out of the way. This one begins to sound like one of those jokes along the lines of "Think of number, divide by 10, add 3, take away 11 and, bingo, you'll find out what the bus driver ate in his sandwiches on Tuesday." Personally I think it's also about as useful and there are better ways of becoming aware of how much you should eat, but if you *really* do want to know what your personal daily calorie burn ought to be, here's what you do. Multiply your weight in kilos by 0.9 and times this by 24. Now multiply this figure by 1.5 if you don't

"If I divide the 2 cream cakes by the 3.5 stops I ran to catch the bus I'd left them on..."

"While you've got your calculator out..." (p.92)

exercise, 1.6 if you exercise less than 3 hours a week, and 1.9 if you exercise for more than 3 hours a week or have an active job. The result tells you how many calories you need to consume each day. If you want to lose 1 pound a week, eat 500 calories less a day. To lose 2 pounds a week, cut back by 1,000, but never go below 1,400 a day. Doing that calculation alone would surely use up at least 100 calories, depending on how hard it was to find a calculator!

What is the reason for your weight issue?

Is being, or feeling, overweight a physical problem? Is it an emotional problem? Or is it a spiritual problem? Body, mind or soul?

I think it's fairly obvious that the answer to the first question is that weight is always a physical problem. You might be overweight because of health reasons such as an underlying medical condition or due to drugs you are required to take for other conditions. Or you may be overweight because you have eaten inappropriate amounts of the kinds of food that make us gain weight and you have combined this with a sedentary lifestyle. Either way, you have a physical problem as a result. It's not just a question of looking good or being vain. Your body was not designed to carry an excessive amount of weight, so even if you have no issues about your size or appearance, your heart, lungs and knees have issues with you carrying all that extra weight. They are straining under the load they are being made to carry. Your body is not working for you as well as it could, so like it or not, you do have a physical problem.

For me a problem arises when it is also suggested that being overweight is automatically a sign of an emotional or spiritual problem. Weight is the accumulation of fat cells. It is *not* a moral or spiritual thing. Yes, I know that being overweight can be linked to low self-esteem and emotional issues, and we will look at all that in a later chapter. But when we make that link, what we are implying is that slim people are emotionally healthy. This is not the case. Skinny people can also be emotional "screw-ups"! At the other end of the scales (excuse the pun), some of the most lovely, funny, kind, intelligent and spiritually switched on people I know are – dare I say it? – fat! Well, they are! There is no point denying it. But I love these people and God loves them too, and neither God nor I are linking their plumptiousness with emotional baggage or spiritual malaise. Yes, they have a physical problem, but we don't need to pile on opprobrium by making any other assumptions.

If you are overweight, I imagine that you may feel like you are living in the middle of a witch-hunt. Hardly a week goes by without a story about the "evil" of obesity. Personally I think a bit of restraint and compassion is needed here. Fat people are *not* evil or lazy, nor are they necessarily even greedy. They do not all suffer from low self-esteem. The real evil of obesity is not the people who suffer it; it is the marketing, advertising and commercial interests of food companies that are really evil. Greg Critser, in *Fat Land: How Americans became the fattest people in the World*,[7] points out that the food industry should carry a huge part of the blame. Back in the 1970s the use of palm oil (a highly saturated fat) and corn syrup (a cheap sweetener) revolutionized the convenience food industry, allowing food to be manufactured more cheaply and have a longer shelf life. We may have come full circle now, with manufacturers selling their products on the basis that they have no saturated fat or all natural ingredients, but they must take some part of the blame for how we got into this state in the first place.

One lady wrote to me the other day lamenting about the size of her tummy. "Most other sins can be hidden", she wrote, "but I carry around the sin of gluttony so that everyone can see." Ouch! That's a really painful way to feel about yourself. Now I don't know this lady well enough to tell you whether she is actually greedy or just has a post-pregnancy bulge. But it disturbs me hugely that she has been made to feel so ashamed of her body shape, as if she is walking round wearing a sandwich-board saying "I'm a sinner". Personally I'm not ashamed of the way pregnancy rearranged my body. My belly carried two beautiful babies, so of course it bulged.

I feel really affronted by this assumption that all weight problems are automatically emotional problems or spiritual problems. I read a Christian book recently about dieting. Three quarters of the book was dedicated to the argument that if you have a weight problem, then *obviously* you have a spiritual problem: either you have low self-esteem or lack of self-discipline or you are a sinful glutton. To me, there is nothing obvious about that connection. I got very, very cross. If I'd been an overweight person reading that particular book, I'd have been even crosser. I would have learned that not only did I have a weight problem (about which I was concerned enough to read or even buy a book), but I also had a spiritual problem. In other words, I wasn't just a fat person; I was also a rubbish Christian. The author promised me that if I resolved my "spiritual issues" through prayer, journalling, accountability and self-control (not "will power" but "God power"), then I would definitely lose weight, without a diet.

Without a diet? Please! Can we get real here?

Calories in, less calories used equals weight gained or weight lost. It's a physical equation. Don't let's over-spiritualize the issue.

Later in this book there will be a whole chapter looking at the emotional issues that do *sometimes* lie behind being overweight, but I would like to emphasize that word "sometimes". If I were pushed I might nudge it up to "often", but let's not go around with the idea that there is *always* an emotional problem behind a weight problem.

So what can you do if you prefer not to diet but you think, or feel, that your weight is an issue? Under the next four headings, I'm going to group loads of tips, each one of which has the capacity to make a big difference. It's not about going on a diet; it's about changing your lifestyle and your approach to food in general.

Eat quality, not quantity

A few years ago a French woman called Mireille Guiliano wrote a book of advice on food called *French Women Don't Get Fat*.[8] Statistically there are far fewer obese people in France and yet they eat three-course meals for lunch, drink wine and indulge in chocolate and delicious little pastries. How do they do it? Eating quality, not quantity, was one of the key principles that Guiliano promoted. In other words, enjoy the widest variety of good food. Examine your diet for what it is that you eat out of all proportion – it could be bread, pastry or maybe chocolate. Don't cut this item out of your diet altogether, for that would be "unsustainable extremism" (the best definition of diet I've ever heard!), but cut it back a little. Realize that most of the pleasure you get from food comes in the first few bites – you don't need to go back for seconds.

She is not alone in recommending that we eat with awareness. Susie Orbach, in her book *On Eating*,[9] agrees that the worst thing we can do is eat without awareness. If we eat slowly and savour every mouthful, two things happen: one, we give our stomach time to send a message to our brains that we are full, and secondly, we are more likely to actually respond to this message by stopping eating because we are less likely to feel resentful. We have enjoyed what we have eaten, we have been aware of the tastes and flavours rather than ramming it down our necks as fast as possible. To this end, Guilano recommends always eating at a table with napkins. Napkins don't have proven weight-reducing properties; they just lend a sense of occasion to a meal! I love the fact that her emphasis is on enjoyment. As I have already said, fear and self-loathing are not good motivators. Anyone who recommends fine wine and good-quality chocolate as daily necessities (both in moderation, of course) sounds good to me. Wine has calories but it also has nutrients; it can lower blood pressure and bad cholesterol. Chocolate contains theobromine which is an appetite suppressant and the cocoa bean is a source of magnesium, one of the nutrients that helps your body burn fat. The bad news is, I'm not talking about the type of milk chocolate bars so readily available at the counters of most stores. These are too high in sugar, palm oil, saturated fat and a host of other unhealthy ingredients. Real chocolate is dark, bitter-sweet and has a high cocoa content of 75 per cent or above. If chocolate is your downfall, try to retrain your taste buds to enjoy real chocolate, and you will find just two squares will give you a better chocolate hit for fewer calories. While we're on the subject, do you eat your chocolate alone? Why? Guilt-ridden secret scoffing is no way to enjoy something. Make it part of life. Enjoy, share; shame-based eating is not a helpful way to go. "Self punishment is not a path to well-being," says Guiliano. Amen to that!

Another way to eat quality, not quantity, is to try to eat food in season. Prepare as much of a meal as possible from fresh ingredients. Try to reduce the amount of pre-processed food in your diet. "Plastic food" or ready meals are made for a long shelf-life, not for a life-enhancing eating experience. I know all this takes time. It represents a huge change of priorities. But food is so much more than a chore that simply keeps me alive; food is an opportunity for conversation and time spent with people I love. I'm honouring my body by taking care over what I eat. Basically I'm expressing my own worth, the worth of others around me, as well as gratitude for the gift of taste and the huge variety of foods available for me to enjoy.

Your appetite is a gift

Most diets work on the assumption that your appetite is the problem. If only we could find a way of overcoming our appetites, then we could control our eating and lose as much weight as we need or desire. But starting out by labelling an important part of ourselves as bad, problematic or uncontrollable is really unhelpful. Instead we need to see our appetite as a gift. We need to embrace the fact that we feel hungry roughly three times a day, and rather than dreading that feeling, as I used to do, we need to welcome it. It's the strongest evidence we have that our body is working well, and if we really learn to listen to our appetites, it's the best guide we have as to what our bodies need.

As I've already said, I've been a "successful dieter" so I know that a certain amount of equipment is necessary to maintain a successful regime: at the very least, a pen and a daily food sheet; possibly a calculator; possibly even a set of scales. What a hassle! And what a relief to realize that I carry around with me all the time, wherever I go, a completely reliable indicator of what and when I need to eat and how much I need to eat. I don't need to weigh anything or work out its value in calories. That indicator is my appetite. Listening to your appetite can be more effective than any points calculator or diet diary. The only problem is that most of us have forgotten how to listen to it. We have become so used to eating for reasons other than hunger. We eat because it's tea time, we eat because we are frustrated, we eat because we feel neglected, we eat because it's there in front of us and we're not paying, we eat for all sorts of reasons other than because we are hungry.

It takes some weeks of conscious retraining to learn to tune into our appetites, but eating when you are hungry and stopping when you are full is actually the only diet advice you ever need. If you were to do that and nothing else, you wouldn't have a weight problem (with the exception of a few medical conditions).

This principle is the essence of Susie Orbach's advice on eating. She proposes that there is a set weight, a size that is right for you, the size your body was meant to be. You can keep to this weight or reach it if you listen to your inner register (your appetite). It will tell you how to eat, when to eat, what to eat and when to stop eating. She offers five "keys": eat when you are hungry; eat the food your body is hungry for; find out why you eat when you aren't hungry; taste every mouthful; stop eating the moment you are full. Others have called this "mindful eating"[10] and suggest asking yourself simple questions such as "Am I hungry?", "Do I really want this?", "Does this even taste good?"

At first glance her plan sounds a little over optimistic and personally, I think if you are several stones overweight, you might need to actually diet first to get nearer your ideal weight. But what she is describing is "how to eat for life", not how to eat for the six weeks of your diet. This is a way of eating you can sustain. It does not cut anything out except mindless grazing. The emphasis is on being conscious of ourselves and conscious of the food we consume.

I wonder if we are actually afraid of the freedom this advice would give us. How much more secure we feel when we know there are rules to follow. The "no pain, no gain" belief is deeply engrained. So we revert to self-deprivation, stalwartly refusing to indulge our cravings when giving in and eating a little of what we fancy probably wouldn't do us any harm. How often have we ended up consuming more calories, in order to make the craving go away, than we would have done if we'd just enjoyed a small serving of whatever it was we fancied in the first place?

Small changes over a long time make a big difference

Here's a whole heap of tips, any one of which could make a huge difference. The key is not to expect instant results but to make a small change in what or how you eat or drink and sustain that change, and you will eventually see a big difference.

Drink more water

You are two-thirds water. Your body needs water to do everything: to get nutrients and oxygen round your body, to flush out waste, to control your temperature. The fastest way to impair your ability to function is to dehydrate. If tea and coffee are the main things you drink, you are probably not getting enough. Plain water is ideal. A mere 2 per cent drop in body water can give you problems with concentration and short-term memory. Drinking plenty of water can ease joint pain. If you are learning to listen to your appetite, you may mistake hunger for thirst. Try drinking water first. A glass of water by your bed will satisfy you if you wake up with the midnight munchies! A glass

" I try to keep my fluid intake balanced but I still feel like a whale! "

"Drink more water..." (p.99)

of water before you eat a meal will mean you'll eat less. Being well hydrated decreases your risk of colon cancer, breast cancer and bladder cancer. I *really* hope you've been to fetch a glass of water during the last paragraph! If I still haven't convinced you, here's a clincher: a German study revealed that after drinking two glasses of water, your metabolism (the rate at which you burn calories) will increase by 30 per cent, and what's more, it will stay that way for an hour.[11] If you don't like the taste of water, train yourself! The adjustment is worth it. Try to avoid even diet drinks, as the artificial sweeteners in these have been shown to induce cravings for more sweetness, so you're more likely to feel like a biscuit after a diet drink, meaning that you'll consume more calories even though you tried to avoid them in the drink.

Sleep more

Tricky, I know, if you have small children or work shifts, but if you do have some control over how long you can sleep, try to get as much as you can. It's been shown that after a bad night's sleep your body will demand more carbohydrates to give it that quick energy burst it needs because you are more likely to feel cold or lethargic. This is a sensible response for a one-off event but a fast way to pile on the pounds if it's a daily occurrence. When you don't sleep your cortisol levels rise. Cortisol is the body's stress hormone. When you are asleep your body is burning fat. When you are awake and active you are more likely to be burning glucose. You probably need to find your own ways to help you get more sleep, but the best generally recommended suggestions are going to bed and getting up at the same time, having a few quiet moments before going to bed, not exercising too close to bedtime and avoiding caffeine.

Plan to stay out of the kitchen

Once you've prepared and eaten a meal, get out of the kitchen. Plan beforehand what you are going to do after a meal so you have reason to move on and move out of the kitchen.

Fill your day with little pleasures, but not all of them calorie related

One of my little pleasures is hand cream. It only takes a moment after washing your hands to pause and rub in some cream. It's not because it's good for my skin (although it probably is); I just like the smell and the texture. Another pleasure is a good cup of coffee. Taking the time to make myself a special coffee or enjoying one in a café is enough of a treat in itself. I can savour it. A cheap, nasty cup of coffee begs for a biscuit as a disguise. If you have a daily treat that does contain calories, choose it carefully. If you want to know what difference that treat would make, divide its calories by ten and the answer you get is the number of pounds you would gain if you ate that item daily for a year. I'm not saying don't eat it, but you may want to compensate in another area if you do.

Eat peanut butter

Yes really! Peanut butter is high in healthy mono-saturated fat (also found in whole nuts, olives and avocados). A study at Harvard University showed that people put on a diet high in this still lost weight but were three times more likely to keep the weight off.[12] Which makes another important point: fat is not the enemy, fat is the element that will make you feel full, so small amounts of healthy fats should be in every meal.

Carry a good snack with you

A bag of nuts or a packet of raisins or something healthy will help tide you over hunger pangs if you are late for a meal or your routine is disrupted. You are more likely to over-eat when you do finally reach food if you have not responded to your appetite earlier. I used to keep a list of healthy snacks inside the kitchen "snack cupboard" door to remind my children what they could eat when they went to "graze" in the kitchen. That way they were making an active choice rather than just eating the first thing they found. The list consisted of "fresh fruit, dried fruit, yogurt, toast, plain popcorn, slice of malt loaf, carrots with dip, cracker with peanut butter, plain biscuit".

Know a bit about what to eat and how much to eat

There are books and books on this, but a good simple guide is the food pyramid: Bread/rice/cereal or pasta, 40 per cent; fruit/vegetables, 30 per cent; dairy, meat or fish, 20 per cent; fats, oils, sweets, 10 per cent. A sensible-sized portion of protein is about the size of your fist.

Get off the sugar rollercoaster

Your body produces energy from the food you eat. Let's just keep it simple by saying that any energy you don't use up immediately gets stored as fat. Carbohydrates are a good way of getting quick energy, so a runner might load up on pasta before a race so that he or she has plenty of quick energy to access. The trouble is that most of us eat like we need quick energy when we actually don't. If we're not running marathons, when we eat too many carbohydrates designed to give us quick energy (i.e. a lot of glucose in our blood), all our bodies can do is convert all that extra energy to fat. The other downside of eating too much carbohydrate is that it will leave us feeling hungry again very soon. So we will swing from feeling low, moody and hungry, have a quick hit such a doughnut, feel better for a short while and then feel as hungry as we did before.

A far better idea is to eat stuff that stays in your tummy for longer. A complex carbohydrate such as wholegrain bread or porridge oats for breakfast is more likely to keep you going till lunch time. (Don't even contemplate not eating breakfast. It's been proven so often that breakfast is not only the most important meal of the day, but people who eat breakfast are less likely to be overweight, due to the fact that they are less likely to reach for mid-morning snacks when their energy flags. Breakfast kick-starts your metabolism, which means calories start getting used up.)

I have found that if I've had periods when I've eaten a lot of carbohydrates (around Christmas time is the worst: cake, mince pies, pastry savouries), it can take about three days to climb off the sugar rollercoaster. In other words, it can take three days to break your sugar addiction, your body's demand for quick hits of easily convertible energy. This is one example where I seem to be contradicting the "listen to your appetite" advice and it's because eating simple carbohydrates will make you want more. Eating fat, on the other hand, will make you feel full. So give careful thought to the question, "What does my body need?" Re-balance your diet by eating more protein. For a couple of days try eating breakfast and lunch with no carbohydrates at all and then eat whatever you want for supper. Three days of this, with no snacks between meals, and you will lose the sugar cravings. Follow this process and it is possible to retrain your palate away from huge bowls of ice-cream and second helpings of crumble.

So making the most of you body, part 1, means tackling the "F" factor. Not fear, nor failure, but learning to enjoy food, to savour every mouthful. "Calories are wasted if they are not tasted."[13] Try to replace the negative food associations with more positive connections: food equals fun, equals friends, equals family and fab times. If that change of attitude feels like too much of a quantum leap for you at the moment, the next factor could be the one that helps you make that change.

NOTES

1.   Susie Orbach, *Bodies*, London: Profile Books, 2009.
2.   N. Hambleton-Jones, *Top to Toe*, London: Mobius, 2008
3.   "Healthy Living Strategy Launched", http://news.bbc.co.uk, 23 January 2008.
4.   Susie Orbach, *Bodies*.
5.   Ibid.
6.   Susie Orbach, *The Guardian*, 10 March 2006.
7.   Greg Critser, *Fat Land*, London: Penguin Books, 2003.
8.   Mireille Guiliano, *French Women Don't Get Fat: the secret of eating for pleasure*, London: Chatto and Windus, 2004.
9.   Susie Orbach, *On Eating*.
10. Joyce Meyer, *Look Great Feel Great*, London: Hodder, 2007.
11. Quoted by Joyce Meyer in *Look Great Feel Great*.
12. Helen Foster, "The Hungry Woman's Diet", *Best Magazine*.
13. P. Cohen and J. Verity, *Lighten Up*, London: Century, 2001.

Chapter 6

Making the Most of Your Body: The "S" Factor

"S" could stand for "svelte" or "superfit", but "sweaty" is what I'm really after. This chapter is all about exercise.

Simply knowing that exercise is really good for you has never been enough to make it popular. Eating sprouts is also good for you, but that doesn't mean we like them. In my experience you either love exercise or you hate it. If you are reading this chapter first, before the rest of the book, then you were probably the captain of the netball team at school. Those naturally gifted, sporty girls who could do triple turns on the trampoline, had washboard stomachs and looked great in short skirts were the bane of my teenage life. This chapter isn't really for them. I'm writing for the rest of us. We wanted to be like them but knew we were worlds apart, so we turned our backs on possibilities of Olympic glory and looked for other ways to excel. Maybe we found them or maybe we didn't, but some of us may have given up on exercise ever since.

The good news is that your attitude to exercise has not been set for life. If you want to change, you can now change how you feel about it. You can find ways to build exercise into your lifestyle so that you will either (a) really enjoy it or (b) hardly notice it, but either way you will really benefit from it. The purpose of this chapter is to help the "less than enthusiastic" or even the "downright resistant" to get up and get active.

My own story is of a change of attitude. After too many cold afternoons on a school hockey pitch wearing thick socks, a short skirt and very dodgy "games" knickers (ours were navy blue), I vowed never again to play any game that involved sticks, mud and cold. I was also sent out on Friday afternoons for cross-country running wearing only those same ghastly knickers and a thin T-shirt that did nothing to keep out the biting wind. I made a similar promise to myself that I would never go running again.

It took me ten years to go back on that promise. I took it up when my children were toddlers. It wasn't so much a case of running in order to get slim or fit. It was more a case of "running away" just to get some space in my head! Their dad would come home sometime around tea time or bath time and I would shove my feet into some trainers and be gone! It wasn't that I didn't enjoy looking after the kids full-time, but after a whole day of walking slowly and bending double I needed to move and stretch and also have some time to myself. I didn't like running, nor was I even good at it; it was simply the easiest thing to do. It was cheap, I didn't have to go to a special location, and freedom was one step outside the front door. To my surprise, I found that if you do something often enough and for long enough, you can improve and even start to enjoy the routine. Being a competitive sort of person, I enjoyed setting myself little goals. The first was to actually run all the way round the block rather than walk and then run. I worked my way up to running for half an hour, then running specific distances. To date my best running achievement was a half marathon, but I achieved that about fifteen years after my first escape through the door in running shoes.

Running remained my main form of exercise through most of my thirties. Once the children started school, it seemed to matter less to have time on my own, so I found a running partner in a good friend. Having someone else committed to run with me ensured I got out regularly when either the weather or my energy levels might have tempted me to stay in. It also meant I stretched myself because she was fitter than I was. The social aspect of a good natter along the way was another huge benefit.

But as I got into my forties I began to realize that running wasn't so great for my joints. My knees and ankles were taking it a bit hard. Not only that, but my friend had moved away and it just didn't hold the same appeal. So I turned back to something I had always loved: riding a bike. Full of happy childhood associations, I remember buying my first adult bike during the first year we were married, but it became a bit of a workhorse with child-seats and trailers, so going out to buy my very own more specialized bike simply for speed was very, very exiting. I'm aware that to anyone who doesn't like cycling I may sound at this point like the strange, sad cycling geek my family say that I am, so I'll try to curb my enthusiasm. Anyway, I do find it hard to put into words why riding a bike is such a joyful thing to do. I love the sense of freedom, the peace and quiet, the scenery, the challenge of getting up hills, the wondering what will be round the corner. Packing a picnic and taking off for the afternoon still thrills me in a completely child-like way. I don't really think of it as exercise.

And I think that's the key. If you don't really like exercise, if you can't see the point of getting hot and sweaty, then you need instead to find something you do enjoy that will get you moving and active. If it isn't either fun or necessary, you're not going to keep it up. So if you can't ever imagine exercise ever being fun for its own sake, then you'll have to find a necessary form of exercise. By this I mean choosing to walk to work or doing several hours of gardening a week. You might enjoy these things, or you might not, but at least doing them will get you moving. (Personally, the only "gardening" I would ever do would be if you dropped me into a jungle and I had to hack my way out. I simply can't see the point, or the appeal, but if it works for you, great!)

More on different types of exercise later. Firstly, I want to give you some good reasons why you should be incorporating exercise into your life. If the whole idea of getting hot and sweaty really doesn't appeal, then clearly you are going to need some solid reasons why you should bother. Here are some brilliant reasons why you should exercise regularly. Notice that almost none of them have got much to do with looking good. Looking good is just a spin-off; there are many other benefits in the long term. So if you thought exercising was just for vain people who want to enhance their physique, think again.

By regular exercise I mean doing something for thirty minutes a day, at least five days a week. Something that raises your heart rate, makes you feel warm, and makes you slightly out of breath. That something could be walking, cycling, swimming, dancing, gardening, skipping, jogging or any number of slightly weirder pursuits, such as hula-hooping or roller blading.

Exercising at that level, you will significantly reduce your chances of having the following illnesses: heart disease, a stroke, diabetes, breast cancer, Alzheimer's, arthritis, asthma, depression and gastro-intestinal ills. You will have fewer colds and less stress, you'll have better muscle tone and should benefit from improved posture, which means your body will hold up better to the ravages of growing older. You'll have muscles which burn fat *all* the time, even while you're sleeping, not just while you are exercising. And the chances are you will sleep better. You'll increase your resting metabolic rate and decrease your resting heart rate, which means you'll burn more calories and pump your blood round more efficiently. Half an hour of moderate exercise on most days has been shown to be as efficient at relieving mild depression as anti-depressants. Exercise triggers endorphins, the chemicals in your brain responsible for good moods. If you are female, your bones will be losing their bone density from your early thirties, but doing a regular weight-bearing exercise as simple as walking can strengthen those bones and significantly reduce your chances of developing osteoporosis. Osteoarthritis, painful inflammation of joints, affects many, if not most, people over sixty, but again it has been shown that keeping moving can significantly reduce the effects. Exercise will boost your immune system. It will help control your blood sugar levels.

Best of all, it's something you can do for yourself, a long-term investment in your own health. So often when we get ill or our bodies fail us in some way, we drag ourselves to a doctor and expect someone else to fix us. Exercise is one way in which we take responsibility for ourselves to prevent ill-health before it strikes.

About twelve years ago I tore a muscle across my shoulder, which left me with chronic neck pain. At my lowest point I was unable to hold a phone up to my ear, lift a kettle or use a computer. Needless to say, it got me really down and the drug regime of sixteen pills a day didn't seem to help. Pain and fear are a toxic combination. Pain leaves you feeling constantly drained and fear leaves you constantly tense, being tense adds to the pain, and as the pain increases, so does your fear, which makes you more tense, and so on and so on. Not so much a vicious circle as a depressing spiral downwards.

Resentment and frustration were probably my dominant emotions at the time. The thing that finally helped me out of that hole was physiotherapy – in other words, exercise! Mind you, going for my initial assessment still rates as one of the most embarrassing experiences of my life. I was assigned not one, but two male physiotherapists, and the first thing they did was have me stand before them in my underwear while they walked around me in silent observation of my "problem" from every angle. Eventually, after what seemed like a very long time, one of them (he was French – I have no idea why that made it feel worse, but it did) said, "Madame, you 'ave veeeery bad posture."

Then they cheerfully strapped my shoulders back. This process placed my shoulder-blades about three feet behind my ears and pushed my boobs about three feet out in front of me – at least that's the way it felt. When the strapping came off after a week, I was prescribed a set of exercises that I was to do three times a day every day for six weeks, without fail. Did I do those exercises? You bet I did! Turning up to see those two "physio-terrorists" once a week pretty much ensured I was going to do my homework. It worked. Movement and exercise was the key to my recovery, although one other significant factor was changing my car from a manual to an automatic.

The whole experience made me a big fan of physiotherapy. It also left me slightly ashamed that I had been so impatient with God for not healing me (I'd been up for prayer many times). When I learnt that a "cure" was in my own hands, I realized that it was my responsibility to take it. There will undoubtedly be health issues in the future that are beyond my power to influence, and when those come I know I'll be praying for healing again. But why should I expect him to help me out if I'm not doing what I can to take care of the body he's given me?

So far I've only listed the physical benefits of exercise. I haven't yet mentioned the social aspect. Exercise can be a great way to make new friends by joining a team or a club. Getting along to the same aerobics class each week can be a good way to make connections with people. Then there are all the emotional benefits: reaching goals, improving fitness and having a toned body can all go a long way to helping you to have a positive body image, to be more self-confident. Becoming aware of what your body can do can make you feel less powerless, more in control of your life, more resilient, even in the face of setbacks.

So don't just sit there! Get that body moving.

Don't groan! Of *course* it's going to feel hard if you haven't exercised in years. It's also going to be challenging if you have a physical condition that limits you in some way. But don't sit there thinking, "Well, I couldn't possibly find the time to exercise for thirty minutes, five days a week", because whatever you can do will still pay dividends. You might not manage to hit that target at first but even a little will help. The principle that we applied to diets in the last chapter applies equally well to exercise: small changes over a long period of time will make a big difference. Say it to yourself as a mantra as you take the stairs rather than the lift, as you park a little further away from the supermarket entrance, as you choose to walk rather than drive.

Rather than focusing on all the negative thoughts that begin, "I can't because…', you need to be telling yourself what an amazing body you already have and learn to celebrate all the incredible things your body is already doing. For example, your eyes blink 5,000 times a day. Each of us has 10,000 times more cells in our body than there are people on the earth. In your life you will shed 20 kilos of skin, the weight of a six-year-old girl, but your skin is constantly renewing itself. Your liver is capable of around 300 functions and is doing all of those things right now without you giving them a moment's thought. If you lost even up to 80 per cent of your liver, it would re-grow (take care of that liver – it's an amazing organ and you've just got the one). Your kidneys filter a litre of blood every minute. Your thigh bone is stronger than reinforced concrete; your jaw muscle can exert a force of 2 tonnes per square centimetre. Your eyes can detect a single photon of light. This is the amount of light that might reach your eye from a candle, one mile away! Your ears contain a bone the size of a grain of rice. The average person's heart will beat about 3 billion times in their lifetime, pumping around 800 million pints of blood. You can expect to breathe 600 million times, enough to fill 400 hot-air balloons. No wonder, then, that inspiration means genius and expiration means death! So much incredible complexity and yet each one of us has spent about half an hour as a single cell.[1] As the psalmist said, "I am fearfully and wonderfully made."[2] All this, and I haven't even touched on temperature regulation, growth, reproduction, digestion, or your amazing brain.

What I'm trying to get over is the fact that your body, regardless of how you feel about it, is an amazing gift. I'm not denying that life is also lived in our minds, where our imagination and intellect help us understand and engage with the world, and also in our emotions where good feelings such as love and acceptance are essential for our well-being. But all it takes is toothache to

"It's not the only thing in there the size of a grain of rice!"

"Your ear contains a bone the size of a grain of rice." (p.112)

remind you that physical discomfort can completely dominate your life. It's almost impossible for us to sustain an intellectual pursuit if we are in physical pain, just as it is also hard for us to maintain emotional equilibrium if we are chronically unwell. If we mistreat or ignore our physical well-being, we hardly have a right to complain if, or more likely when, our body lets us down.

So with all that in mind and given that this isn't an exercise handbook, I'm going to just briefly touch on four activities that are simple enough for anyone to try: walking, running, cycling and swimming.

Walking

Walking is an activity that can raise your energy levels, improve your mood and lower your weight, all without dieting – no small claim. But the occasional stroll is not going to achieve all that. If you were to walk for forty-five minutes four times a week, you would lose 18 pounds of weight in a year, without any changes to your diet.[3] Not bad for an activity that is costing you next to nothing. All you need is a good pair of shoes.

The equipment is often not the off-putting bit, it's the time factor. I would suggest trying to build up the time spent walking gradually, starting with just ten minutes, or break down the thirty-minute walk into a couple of shorter walks. Is there a way you can build this into your day, either as part of your journey to work or in your lunch hour?

Maybe one way of motivating yourself to walk would be to join a group, or treat yourself to a walk in a beautiful place such as a nearby beauty spot or park. The combination of open green spaces and physical activity is as near magical as you can get when it comes to lifting depression. If, even after all I've said about health benefits, you either still can't see the point or can't be cured of your Protestant work ethic, maybe you could enter a charity walk and use that as your target. That way you'll be able to say, "I'm not being self-indulgent, I'm in training."

Once you've actually got out the door in a decent pair of shoes, it would be worth spending the first few minutes of your walk walking slowly to warm up. Then, as you pick up the pace, remind yourself of the way you are walking. I know you've been walking for a long time now but it's amazing how a little self-awareness can make a big difference. If you tighten your core muscles (tummy, bottom and pelvic floor) you'll get much more benefit from your walk in terms of improving your posture. Walk tall with your shoulders back, chin level with the ground and head centred (i.e. not jutting out or tilted back). Relax your shoulders down and back. As you speed up don't lengthen your stride, take shorter steps faster. Bend your arms and move the arm opposite to the leg that's forward to move your waist, but don't swing your arms as this will tend to make you sway your hips. Keeping your hips level will be better for your knees. On the subject of knees, the use of walking poles has seemed much more in vogue recently and not just for serious walkers going up and down mountains. Certainly poles do make a huge difference for gradients of either direction because they will significantly reduce the load on your knees. Your pole (or poles) should be adjusted so that when it touches the floor you are comfortably gripping the handle with your elbow at a right angle. But don't be put off walking because you haven't got poles; they hardly seem necessary for a brisk fifteen-minute walk around the block! Buy some poles once you're ready for some day walks or climbs.

Running

Everything I've already said about walking pretty much applies to running, except for the bit about poles. The bit about starting gently and building up slowly is even more important. One reason most people give up is because they have gone at it too hard and too fast and end up in pain. Run at a pace at which you can hold a conversation (take a buddy or you'll look silly talking to yourself!). You will need slightly more equipment: a decent pair of trainers and a good sports bra. If you are well endowed, it is particularly important that you keep your boobs in one place. Once you stretch the ligaments that support them, they stay stretched, and you don't want to accelerate the rate at which your bosom gravitates south. Age will accomplish that feat for you, so if you have anything more than a B cup invest in an industrial-strength sports bra before you take up running.

Your first target is to run for just ten minutes. Begin by walking briskly and then break into a gentle jog, but don't worry if you can only maintain that for two or three minutes. If you go out every other day or every third day, you'll soon be running for ten minutes. Once you've reached ten minutes of running, you can build it up by increasing it for a minute or two every third session. This is a really gentle rate of increase but the key fact is that it is achievable. You will be less likely to suffer injuries or stiffness if you build up slowly.

The other reason most people give up is because something comes along to break their "habit" – either they have a busy week, or they miss a run because it was raining or for some other reason. Having a "bad patch" and not getting out does make it harder to get going again, but it won't undo all the work so far so long as you do get going again. If you sleep badly for a couple of nights, you don't give up on sleeping, do you? Quite the reverse; you know it's essential, so you might try to get a couple of early nights to make up for your lack. Exercise is no less essential than sleeping. Inevitably something will come along to break your rhythm or habit, but don't let that put you off altogether.

You will reach a point when not only do you enjoy going out, you will keenly feel the lack if you miss the chance of exercise. Things that will help get you to this point and sustain you are: listening to music (some upbeat tracks on an iPod or an MP3 player can make a huge difference to keeping up a good pace); going with a friend (as you are less likely to back out); varying your route and trying to include some green places and also some changes of gradient. To get more "value" from your half-hour investment of time, vary your pace. I particularly liked to sprint when I knew I was five minutes from home, putting every last ounce of energy into that last stretch, but actually, interval training, where you go faster and then slower in intervals, increases the benefits of your run.

Other things you will find helpful as you improve are running shorts or trousers, a light-weight breathable waterproof, a hat and some gloves for the winter, and a water bottle that's easy to hold. Again, if you need some external motivation, there are many charity runs you can enter, not just marathons or half marathons. After six weeks' training most people could work up to a five-kilometre distance, and if you have built running into your lifestyle for six weeks, the chances are you will be motivated to keep going after your target event.

Cycling

All four of these activities are aerobic. In other words, they are good for your heart and lungs. Walking and running are slightly more weight bearing and will be more challenging for your joints, but so long as you build up slowly you shouldn't have any difficulties. Cycling and swimming are slightly easier on your joints. Both will give you a good cardiovascular workout and both will increase muscle strength, but cycling is particularly good for endurance and swimming is excellent for increasing flexibility.

Cycling is perhaps the easiest form of exercise to fit into your day if you can use your bike as your main form of transport. Most car journeys are under two miles – that's only fifteen minutes on a bike. Some two-mile car journeys can take fifteen minutes if you are stuck in traffic. And using your bike is not only good for you, it's good for the environment.

People who say they don't like cycling have usually not been on the right bike. Often they have only ever ridden a mountain bike and decided all bikes are the same. They are not. Mountain bikes are the 4x4 equivalent in the cycling world – great if you want to bounce along bumpy mountain tracks but hard work if you are going along an ordinary road. Having the right bike for what you want to do is vital, as is having that bike set up to fit you. Your toes should just be able to touch the floor when you are on the saddle; you should be able to have your elbows bent and rest your hands on the handlebars. Broadly speaking, an ideal everyday bike would be a hybrid bike or a road bike. A hybrid is somewhere between a mountain bike and a road bike. It might have suspension (which means you feel the bumps less but makes you go a bit slower because it absorbs some of your effort) and wider tyres but without the chunky tread of a mountain-bike tyre. A hybrid is ideal for either a commute or a long day ride or for touring. Last year I loaded up my hybrid with two panniers and cycled from the Midlands to John O'Groats over eleven days. It did the job just fine but if I'd had one with an aluminium frame this would have been even better as the bike itself would have been lighter. A road bike is a very light bike with a rigid frame (i.e. no suspension). It is designed for speed and will have skinny tyres with very little tread. They are not great on uneven surfaces but are fantastic if speed is what you are after. All of these bikes have gears, usually 21 or 24, so hills don't have to feel so hard. You can even get a super-low gear fitted which makes going uphill slow but painless.

In the UK there are some fantastic cycling routes that are mostly on very quiet roads or cycle tracks, so don't let the traffic put you off. There is also a wealth of cycling groups you can join or timed events at weekends if you want to go against the clock.

I find the pace of a bike ride is just about perfect. If I'm walking I will quickly get bored with the scenery but on a bike, there's always the next corner to turn or hill to crest and you're looking at a different view. You can also cover a decent distance quite quickly but it's very easy to stop for a snack, a rest or to admire the view.

It's true that cycling definitely involves more equipment, the bike itself being the most important item. Things that will help you keep going are: a water bottle or water reservoir in a backpack, panniers, a cycle computer that will tell you your speed and distance, a cycle helmet, some reflective clothing, clips if your wear trousers and cycling gloves with padding. Apart from the computer all of these are pretty much essential, especially the gloves. If you cycle long distances without them the pressure will affect the nerves in your hand and you may lose some sensation in your fingers temporarily. If your wrists get sore you could experiment with different handlebars or add hand-grips that allow you to change your hand position. Drop-down handlebars have always felt too scary for me; besides, I like to cycle with my head up. But you need to see what feels right for you. The important thing is to have the seat at the right height. At the lowest part of the push on the pedal your leg should be almost but not completely extended. You should be pushing on the front of your foot and your handlebars should be roughly level with your seat. If your knees seem particularly sore you might want to invest in some proper cycling shoes. These don't flex in the middle like walking shoes and somehow they take some strain off your knees.

Basically a bike can be adjusted in hundreds of ways so don't give up until it feels right for you. Some people would have added cycling shorts with padding to the list of essentials, but unless you are doing long distances you can get away without them so long as you have a good saddle. Cycling shorts should more accurately termed cycling underpants because if you wear anything underneath your shorts you'll seriously increase your risk of chafing. If you feel dreadfully uncool or exposed in cycling shorts, you could always wear them under a loose pair of ordinary shorts.

One last idea for would-be cyclists who don't fancy the bad weather or the traffic: try a spinning class. These have become very popular and consist of cycling to music on stationary bikes in a class setting at a leisure centre or health club. It's not half as boring as it sounds. If the instructor is good you will be pushed to vary your pace and resistance to simulate racing or going up hills, and after forty-five minutes you will have had a very thorough work-out. This can be a great way to keep cycling fit in the winter if you prefer getting out on your bike in the better weather. (Warning: ten minutes into your first class and you will think you are going to die! The likelihood is you will get over that point, but these classes do vary in intensity, so ask when you book. Start with the easiest level and the least resistance.)

Swimming

Swimming has all the benefits of aerobic exercise with the added bonus that you're not aware of getting sweaty. It is also very good for increasing flexibility, especially in the shoulder area. It will tone the upper body far more than either cycling, running or walking. In terms of equipment and cost, you obviously need a costume and the pool entrance fee or membership. A good pair of goggles is also an essential. If you were to do breast stroke for prolonged periods, keeping your head lifted out of the water, you will be putting a lot of strain on your neck. You would be much better off wearing goggles and putting your face in the water at each stroke. This obviously means getting your hair wet so if that's an issue, get a swimming cap. Ideally you should vary the strokes you do to give you the best overall work-out.

Assuming you are swimming indoors, the weather will never be an excuse not to go. The only downside that I can see is boredom. Also I haven't yet found a pair of goggles that don't leave me looking like a panda for several hours after. But now I am influencing you with my prejudices. The fact is that swimming may be for you the most convenient, ideal form of exercise.

Beating boredom

One of the best ways to keep your interest in exercise is to vary your routine. Rather than just doing one of the above, why not try to include each activity into a weekly routine? Or if cycling is more appealing in the summer, try to swim more in the winter. By introducing this kind of variety you'll be using a wider range of muscle groups and be at less risk of injury or strain from one repeated form of exercise. But by far the best way to avoid boredom is to make exercise a social activity. It would be good to think about your personal preferences before you decide how to do this. Are you a competitive person who'd like to join a team or take part in a league? In which case, look out for a women's netball team or a squash league. If you're more solitary and less competitive, then simply inviting a friend to go out for a walk might be all that it takes.

Another way to vary your routine is to regularly switch your aerobic training for a session of strength training or flexibility training. These two forms of exercise will not make you hot and sweaty or out of breath. Strength training is sometimes called resistance training or weight training, which makes most of us think about those weight machines in the gym. Generally you need to be shown how to sit on these contraptions and what to pull, squeeze or lift. It all feels a bit inelegant to me and I think many women are put off by the complexity of these machines. The idea of building up a lot of muscle mass also fails to appeal, so women often ignore strength training. This is a real shame because strength training with weights is brilliant. The fact is, it doesn't actually need such a lot of fancy equipment. Doing a few simple exercises holding tins of baked beans also qualifies! Mini sets of dumbbells or elastic resistance bands are a little more dignified but the principle is the same. You are lifting or pushing/pulling against a weight or resistance band with a view to strengthening your muscles. Generally this sort of training covers eight to ten exercises, each one working a particular muscle group, and these exercises are done as sets of repeats. But let me tell you something really encouraging: you don't need to exercise all eight muscle groups everyday. In fact I have recently discovered that doing *just two* sets of exercises a day with a quick warm up and few stretches afterwards makes a *huge* difference. I have been doing this for about six weeks now and it has done more to change my shape than hours of aerobic exercise ever did. I am now a huge fan of strength training.

For example did you know that if you do aerobic exercise your metabolism will be raised for just a few hours afterwards. After doing strength training exercises your metabolism will work harder for the next twenty-three hours, burning more fat for all that time. What's more it only takes fifteen minutes every day to do two sets of exercises including the the warm up and stretches. Fifteen minutes? That's not much is it? Actually the book that inspired me was called *8 Minutes in the Morning*[4] but I've never managed it that fast!

I didn't intend to lose weight when I started strength training because I

"And bend and stretch and lift ... and relax"

"You are lifting or pushing/pulling..." (p.120)

didn't actually need to but a lot of skirts and trousers that were a bit too tight now fit comfortably. My shape has actually changed, with no dieting and not very much aerobic exercise. My job has recently changed and now I only have time to cycle to and from work, only a couple of miles each way, about four or five times a week. In addition to this my back ache has gone and I'm not so frightened about hurting my neck when I lift things because I know my arms are stronger.

I do this routine six mornings a week: on day one I will exercise my chest and back muscles, the next day will be shoulders and abs, then the next day triceps and biceps, then calves and quads, then hamstrings and buttocks, then inner and outer thighs. The sneaky thing about this routine is that only one part of your body will ache at any time! And you *will* ache. When I first started I got up every morning knowing exactly which bits I'd exercised the day before. Now I've been going through my routine for this long, I can see real progress. Some exercises felt near-on impossible at the outset because for example my chest and arm muscles were very weak but now I can manage the full four repeated sets and might even add extra weight or resistance in order to keep challenging those muscles. There's nothing more motivating than progress!

Let's put one worry aside: a resistance training regime will not give you bulging muscles. Your female hormones will automatically cap how much muscle mass you will develop, but the idea is to develop at least some muscle mass, because muscles use up more calories than fat and muscles equal strength. This is really important for women because we are much weaker in relation to our body weight, which means that as we get older we are at greater risk of losing the ability to perform physical tasks easily. An inactive adult will lose about 5–7 pounds of muscle every decade, so an inactive fifty year old has 15–20 pounds less muscle than she did at twenty. Loss of muscle is what partly accounts for weight gain and the higher prevalence of disability and falls among elderly women.[5]

Put simply, flexibility training is stretching. Activities such as Yoga and Pilates are largely flexibility training. They are very important when it comes to maintaining the range of movement in our joints. There are static stretches (which is when you ease into a position and hold it) and dynamic stretches (where you might repeat a simple action). If you join a class for any aerobic activity, the chances are the instructor will guide you through some warm-up and cool-down stretches before and after the activity. These exercises can be very helpful to do on their own, particularly first thing in the morning or last thing at night or when you get up from your computer desk or while you wait for the kettle to boil. If you suffer from low back pain or carry stress in your neck and shoulders, it would be a valuable investment of your time to learn some simple stretches.

If all this is beginning to sound scarily serious, don't be put off. Take a look at your current lifestyle. How active are you anyway? You may already be fitting in two sessions' worth of exercise a week by doing the garden or walking to work. All it takes is a little creativity to carve out some time for two more. Think of the health benefits and the social benefits; maybe there will also be benefits for your family. Can you find a way to exercise with your spouse or children so you are spending time with them and setting a good example at the same time? (How virtuous can you get!) Personally, I dragged both my kids on long-distance cycle rides and neither has ridden a bike much since! Oh well, some you win, some you lose. Research in America has shown a direct correlation between the amount of TV a child watches and the likelihood of the child being obese. The single most effective way for children to lose weight is not actually a diet or exercise routine, it is to reduce TV viewing.[6] The risk is not just the fact of being sedentary; the other factors are the TV snacking and the effect of adverts. One idea is to make TV viewing a chosen activity, not a "default" activity – that is, choose to turn it on and off for a particular programme, but don't turn it on to simply "channel surf". If changing your children's viewing habits feels like redirecting a tidal wave, start by reviewing your own habits. Being willing to offer an alternative activity that involves time spent with you is harder work but could have benefits all round, particularly if that activity involves some exercise. If you claim not to have time to exercise but you have time for two or three hours watching the TV or surfing the Net, you need to ask yourself how much you really want to be fit.

At the beginning of this chapter I said that I didn't think your attitude to exercise was set for life, that you could develop a more positive outlook *if you want to*. The last four words in the previous sentence might be the most important factor in the equation. For you they represent the ten-foot-high wall you feel you'd have to scale to ever enjoy an active lifestyle. It may be that the "I can't" or "I'll fail" sentences that run through your head are way more powerful than any of the motivations and incentives I've tried to offer in this chapter. In the final two chapters of this book I will be looking at those internal self-defeating and self-destructive messages and beliefs and how we can recognize and disarm them. Before that there is one final factor that will go a long way to helping us feel body confident, and it has nothing to do with diet or exercise and everything to do with shopping.

Bring it on!

NOTES

1. All these facts were gleaned from Steve Parker, *The Human Body Book*, London: Dorling Kindersley, 2007, and Deepak Chopra, *Magical Mind, Magical Body*, Niles, IL: Nightingale-Conant, 2000.
2. Psalm 139:14.
3. Dr James Rippe, *The Complete Book of Fitness Walking*, New York: Prentice Hall Press, 1989
4. J. Cruise & A. Robbins, *8 Minutes in the Morning*, Ashford: Rodale Books, 2001.
5. Fiona Hayes, *Multi-sport Training for Fitness*, London: A&C Black Publishers, 2004.
6. Oliver James, *Affluenza*, UK: Vermilion, 2007.

Chapter 7

Making the Most of Your Body: The "P" Factor

"P" is for presentation, and this chapter is all about how we present ourselves. Presentation covers all the subtle skills of clever dressing and the careful use of make-up. Self-enhancement also includes styling your hair and looking after your body in any number of ways which might include defoliation, exfoliation and moisturization, or in other words stripping, scrubbing and slapping stuff on. It's all fabulously girly and faintly self-indulgent and might feel to some women frankly too much of an effort or too much of an exercise in deceit. If your ambivalence about looking good is for either of those reasons, I hope to help you see it doesn't have to be that much of an effort and it's not about trying to be something you're not – it's all about making the most of who you are.

It kind of goes without saying that you're only going to want to present yourself well if you believe "you are worth it", to quote a well-known slogan.

"Don't you come that holier than thou
attitude with me!"

"Looking a frump is not a virtue." (p. 129)

But there are some women whose appearance and apparel give out clearly the message, "I'm rubbish, don't look at me, I feel worthless and I'm not worth the effort." If you'd put yourself in this group, you might be better reading the following chapter first and coming back to this one.

Most of us go along with the whole self-enhancement idea at least a little way. Most of us know clothing can be used to good effect, but we still feel confused by all the latest trends, uncertain about what would look good on us and fearful of getting it wrong. So we either stick to our safe favourites or we feign indifference, or we do both. The fact is that a little bit of knowledge can go a very long way, and investing some time or money acquiring that knowledge could have a huge impact in terms of confidence, as well as saving you a shedload of money that you might otherwise have spent on colours and styles that simply didn't suit you.

Careful self-presentation and grooming is not an exercise in deceit, it's about making the best of your shape and features. It does not make you trivial, shallow or ostentatious. Looking a frump is not a virtue and does not make you more virtuous either. Looking good and feeling confident and comfortable in your clothes is much more likely to make you less self-conscious rather than more.

In the survey I carried out for this book, clothing was the single most suggested way of living with or compensating for almost any unacceptable aspect of our appearance. Every option from "wear bright colours" or "baggy/ flowing clothes" to "avoiding sacks" was suggested. Although when you were supposed to do one and avoid the other was gloriously inconsistent. This suggests a strong degree of confusion over exactly how to use clothes to look your best. A fair summary of the advice I collected would be: loose clothes were for hiding in, tailoring was for disguising bits you didn't like and low-cut tops were for distracting attention!

It's easy to get confused. You can buy any number of books that will tell you exactly what to wear or "what not to wear" for whatever problem you feel you have. If you have a big bust there are some helpful rules to follow. If you have short legs there are another set of guidelines. Similarly, if you have a flabby tummy, there are some styles that will help disguise it, but I haven't yet found a guide that tells you what to wear if you have short legs, a flabby tummy *and* a big bust! In other words, few of us fit neatly into one category or another. So I've just read that if I have a big butt I'm supposed to avoid A line skirts – OK, that sounds easy, I can do that. But then I read that if I have wide hips I'm supposed to wear an A line skirt! Forgive me for sounding thick, but surely if I have a big butt I'm likely to also have wide hips? So which kind of skirt should I wear? A line, straight, pencil, tailored, bias cut, high waisted, low waisted? Soon our heads are in a spin and we end up buying any old skirt because (a) it's our favourite colour, (b) it's cheap or (c) we've always worn this style. Only the brave or the well informed can get round this dilemma.

I would like to think that by the end of this chapter you will be both braver and better informed. But due to the infinite variety of body shapes out there, I can only tell you so much. Sometimes the best I can hope to do is signpost you to better sources of information, but I hope I can at least convince you that these would be worth following up.

Of course, presentation doesn't just cover clothes. It also includes accessories and personal grooming, which in turn might include beauty treatments – anything from algae wraps, face packs and haircuts. Nothing complicated about a haircut… you'd think. Everyone will get their hair cut from time to time; the tricky bit is to know what style will suit you, and then there are decisions to be made about colour. Even so, this is still relatively straightforward when you compare it to beauty products and treatments. Are they necessary? Helpful? Worth the money? Take, for example, a "Detoxifying Algae Wrap". Not in fact a sandwich but an hour's treatment in a beauty salon. It sounds wonderful in the brochure: "a therapeutic, balancing, detoxifying treatment involving skin brushing, gentle exfoliation and algae envelopment rich in minerals and enzymes". It promises to boost my metabolism and speed up the elimination of toxins. Now why do I feel a sudden, irrational need to spend more than our weekly grocery bill paying to be scrubbed down with seaweed? Will I look any different afterwards? Do I really have toxins that need eliminating? Or am I just being a sucker for slick advertising?

The whole area of beauty products and beauty treatments is a minefield of choice. It would really help to know what works and what is a waste of time and money. The advertisers are clearly not going to tell you that and I can only offer you my view, but I'm very aware that what I'm offering is my subjective opinions born out of personal experiences. So I promise not to judge you if you choose to spend *"How much?!"* on acrylic nails, and you must promise not to judge me for my shortcuts and "make do"s. I'd like for us both to look good and feel great without losing our souls in the process. And I am convinced that looking good matters, so sometimes you have to pay a bit. Some days I do feel very "high maintenance" and wish I'd married a Jew because, apparently, they are meant to give their wives a monthly allowance purely for cosmetics, perfumes and self-enhancement! As it is, I have a lingering guilty feeling about the disproportionate amount spent on my appearance as opposed to his. But then I think, "Well, he enjoys looking at me, so it's not like he doesn't benefit!"

And looking good is not as superficial as it seems. It can have a profound impact on how we feel about ourselves. I remember a tearful conversation with a new mum. Since she was no longer bringing in an income, her husband had suggested she should economize by spending less money having her hair done. What he'd overlooked was the fact that the highlights in her hair weren't just a fashion statement, they were more of a survival statement: "I'm still an attractive woman, I'm still me, I'm not just a mum with bags under my eyes, milk stains on my blouse and vomit over one shoulder." I could argue that there are few times in life when a good hair-do is more important!

Clothes

I admit that I often suffer from the "what to wear" dilemma, otherwise known as the "I haven't got anything to wear" dilemma. On a special occasion, if I haven't given it enough thought in advance, getting dressed will involve seven, ten or even fourteen items coming out of the wardrobe, being tried on, then being discarded on to the bed. The whole process can take anywhere between twenty-five and forty-five minutes, but because I don't like deciding what to wear, I tend to leave it to the last minute. So with five minutes to go before we're due to leave, David will come into the bedroom to find a clean shirt and a smart pair of shoes (such difficult decisions) and find me changing colour faster than a traffic light. Usually by the time I am ready we're so late that David has lost the will to live and definitely the ability to compliment me on my choice of outfit.

There is a very good case to be made for having a capsule wardrobe. That's not a very small piece of furniture but the phrase used to describe having a limited set of clothes, each one of which goes perfectly well with any of the other items. I haven't yet reached such heights of organization. But I have taken the first and most important step towards co-ordination – I have had my "colours" done.

Learning what colour suits your skin tone, hair colour and eye colour can be an absolute revelation. You can read any number of books that will try to describe what combinations of skin tone and eye colour constitute "cool"or "warm", but I would wholeheartedly recommend putting yourself in the hands of someone professionally trained. It will be worth every penny. It will cost quite a lot of pennies but it will more than pay you back in terms of wasted purchases. It is not as obvious or easy to self-diagnose your own colour preferences as you might think. Usually a colour consultant will sit you in front of a mirror and drape differently coloured scarves around your neck until they find the season or palette of colours that suits you best. I am a "winter". I suit strong, cool colours. I look truly terrible in virtually any shade of brown and beige makes me look like a corpse. Apart from that I can wear virtually any colour, but it's important to choose the right shade of that colour, and when I left my consultation I was given a handy wallet of "my" best colours. Make sure that this carry-away element is also part of any consultation you book. If you are an "autumn", you will look completely dreadful in black but you will come alive in rusty reds, warm browns, khaki and olive. "Summers" and "springs" have different shades again but don't worry if your consultant doesn't use the seasons to define your category; there are a number of different systems out there but they all boil down to understanding the difference between a warm colour and a cool one, bright or soft shades and whether you suit deep or lighter shades.

As a teenager I spent a large amount of time in brown, beige and apricot because it was what was in fashion and I didn't really have the courage or confidence to go for the brighter colours. Thankfully I did choose a pure white wedding dress (more by luck than judgement), as cream would have been a disaster on me. In fact, if you really can't afford a colour consultation, have a friend round and try on a pure-white T-shirt and then a cream one. Stand in natural light and get your friend to help you decide which one does the most for you. Pure white is "cool". If it suits you, it will have an uplifting effect, lighting up your eyes. However, if it's not your colour it will make you look "washed out". Try on the cream T-shirt; if its warm tones make your skin glow, then you know you need to wear warm colours (colours without a blue undertone). There are plenty of books probably even in your local library that

"I'll put up with 'colour m'lud beautiful' but I draw the line at having the dock feng shui'd"

"Learning what colour suits your skin tone..." (p.132)

will explain which colours work well together, but a personal consultation will remove all doubt from your self-diagnosis.

After colour, the second most important element of choosing the right clothes is shape: your shape and the shape of the clothes you're wearing. There are loads of guidelines addressing different body shapes and imbalances, so I realize I am at risk of over-simplifying things in such a brief chapter. But even if we can only keep half a dozen helpful tips in our head when we go shopping, they may be enough to save us from being seduced by special offers or returning to safe, familiar options. Whether it suits us is far more important than whether it's in fashion or a good price, so following the rules that work for our shape should be our first consideration.

So let's start with our feet and work up.

Shoes

Always wear the same depth of colour as your lower garment. Don't put a bright colour on something you don't wish to emphasize, so if you don't want anyone to notice your size eight feet, don't wear pink clogs! If you feel you have fat ankles, don't wear a sandal with an ankle strap as it will draw attention to the thickness of your ankle. In winter a pair of long boots that fit snugly around the ankle will slim you down. If you have short legs you can make them look longer by wearing the same colour all the way down your legs – the same colour socks and shoes or tights and heels. Another trick for short legs is to wear either court shoes or shoes with open toes, as a shoe that reveals more of your foot makes your legs seem longer.

Trousers

These should be long enough to cover your shoes if you have short legs. If you have thick calves and ankles or short legs, never wear cropped trousers – they will make your legs look shorter and stop at the thickest part. Tapered trousers, ones that go down to a narrow ankle, are almost always a bad idea, but particularly if you are pear-shaped with a bigger backside and wide hips. You want wide trousers that will fall straight down off your hips or trousers that will flare at the bottom to balance the width at the top. Don't wear trousers with pleats at the front unless you are very slim; the pleats are not there to be filled. If you are a bit flabby round the middle, the best type of trousers would be flat fronted with a side zip. As for details, try not to put small things in big places

– for example, small pockets on the back of jeans can just make your backside look bigger. If you have a waist, put your waist-band on it but be aware that high-waisted trousers can make a big bottom larger. The trick with wide hips and big butts is to balance them with the shoulders and emphasize the waist if you've got one.

Skirts

I'm not sure I can resolve the A-line dilemma. They are generally good for a straight figure shape but basically an A-line skirt that stops at your knees will also slide over a big butt. However, if your butt isn't that big, just moderately shapely, it will also look good in a tailored fitted skirt or a flared skirt that kicks out at the bottom and balances the shape of your bottom. If you have short legs, don't wear a skirt with a dropped waistband; it will instantly make your legs look even shorter. As to fabrics, don't wear soft clingy fabrics or bias-cut skirts if you don't want to emphasize your shape. Generally you should put the lighter colours and patterned fabrics on the parts of your body to which you wish to draw attention.

Dresses

When it comes to prints, think about proportion: a small print for petite sizes, a moderate print for average sizes and a large print for big girls. A tailored dress is best for someone with not much of a waist, and another thing that works is wearing a dress that falls from under their boobs (the empire line). If you have bigger boobs you can get away with a low-scoop neck, not to show off cleavage but to show some space between your neck and your boobs. Without this space your boobs can look like they start at your neck. Also for big boobs, go for a design that separates them, like a wrap dress or a V-neck to avoid them looking like a shelf on your upper body. A halter neck, spaghetti straps or high round necks are not good looks for anyone blessed with a voluptuous bosom or bigger upper arms. If you are small and skinny without many curves (i.e. no boobs to speak of) you will want to buy a dress that is shaped and well tailored. Hold it up on the hanger and ask yourself whether or not it looks like it's already got a body in it. If it falls like a sack, put it back. Small, skinny girls with no boobs can wear halter necks, high necks and polo necks and blouses with plenty of frill, froth and detail on the chest to make up for what's not there. An empire-line top or dress isn't great for a girl with small boobs. If that's you, you should also avoid anything with a low-scoop neck because it creates too much empty space. A V-neck or a wrap top will better create the illusion of curves. A V-neck also looks good on big-breasted women, with the proviso about cleavage above. A top or dress that hugs your middle but is loose around your breasts will also minimize your assets. Basically don't put them in anything shiny and tight fitting. As for dress length, if you have short legs you would look good wearing a dress over trousers, but for a dress on its own, make sure the hem comes no lower than just below the knee. Women with short legs can wear calf-length skirts or dresses but only with high-heeled boots of the same colour which will give the illusion of longer legs.

Coats and jackets

If you haven't got much of a waist, a well-tailored jacket or coat can instantly create one for you. Wear the coat open and tie the belt at the back if it has one. If you are an apple shape, don't wear anything double breasted – it'll make you look wider – and don't wear a belt on your coat, which will look like a strap round a fridge. A funnel or round neck-line will add to a bulky, square shape. If you are broad shouldered or busty you need a V-neck coat. Women with no waist might want to try a wide belt worn round the hips. If you have short legs you would look good in a three-quarters length jacket over trousers or a long-line jacket that ends just under your bum. Jackets should end here if you're trying to disguise a bigger bottom. The basic rule is that the hem of the garment will draw your eye, so you don't want this cutting across your widest part. If you are well endowed in the boob department, make sure your jackets are tailored, with narrow lapels and definitely not double-breasted (goodness, you've got enough already – surely that makes sense!).

T-shirts and tops

If you've got big arms always wear sleeves. Long floaty sleeves with fluted open cuffs will balance your upper arms. Even T-shirts with cap sleeves will be better than no sleeves. Avoid puff sleeves if you have big arms, except for a puff on the shoulder seam, which will add more fabric around the arm, creating the illusion that there's not much flesh underneath. Fat arms in tight sleeves can look like sausages in skins. The exception to this might be a three-quarter-length sleeve if you have narrow forearms and wrists you'd like to emphasize. Wrap-around T-shirts are great for creating shape and ruching can disguise a flabby tummy. Just be careful where the hem falls on a wrap cardigan if you don't want to emphasize your bum. If you have a rectangular shape you are better in a square or V neck. In my opinion, I don't think the ordinary T-shirt shape with a high, round neck does a lot for most of us. It's the default T-shirt shape, and if we thought harder we could probably find a style that does more for our shape.

Jewellery

If you have a short neck, wearing dangly earrings can make it look longer. Choker necklaces as well as turtle- or polo-neck tops are also out for you. A shirt with a collar turned up will enhance your neck. If you have big boobs and a short neck, you should wear something delicate around your neck but not on your boobs, as that would make them look bigger (remember what I said about small things in big places). Girls with bigger boobs can wear big chunky necklaces but they need to be worn between your boobs. Smaller girls with flat chests can get away long necklaces (think 1920s).

Underwear

Perhaps I should have started with this category of clothing, as decent underwear is the foundation of all your other outfits. The thing to say about bras is that it is worth getting yourself properly measured every time you invest in a bra. And a bra should be an investment; don't skimp on cheap bras. It should fit you tightly round the ribcage; you should only be able to get one finger under the strap. It is the tightness around your ribs that gives the uplift, not the straps. The straps are there to hold your boobs in the right place. A plain bra in a smooth fabric will be more versatile than a lacy affair and if you are large breasted, you particularly want a smooth profile but also a bra that separates – you don't want a solid shelf of bosom across your front. Anyone above a D cup should be in under-wired bras, but actually, if you're only a B cup a bit of under-wiring can do a lot to raise your assets. Underwear can work "miracles": small boobs can have cleavage, saggy butts can be made pert again, tummies can be smoothed and panty lines eliminated. These last effects are largely achieved by the "magic pants" style of corset or figure-hugging undies. Whatever you do, if you are wearing these do not leave it till the last minute to go to the loo! The other miracle of lingerie is simply that it makes you feel better. Wearing matching pants and bras has a curious effect; you might be the only one who knows how coordinated you are underneath, but that inner knowledge somehow makes a difference to your overall confidence. Come to think of it, that is the essence of everything I've been trying to say in this book; think of good lingerie as a parable!

Belts and scarves

If you are not a chunky girl, don't wear a chunky belt buckle – it'll swamp you. If there's not a lot of you between your boobs and your butt, don't fill it with a wide belt. As to colour, if you are wearing one colour all over, don't break it up with a differently coloured belt. Remember that the belt will draw attention wherever you put it, so don't wear it on your widest part. A short neck needs narrower scarves but a long neck can get away with a thick scarf looped round to make a polo-neck effect. A scarf softens an older wrinkly neck brilliantly and if you get the colour right, it should lighten up your face, not overwhelm it.

Armed with all this information, you should be able to shop with confidence but, if not, some larger department stores do offer a personal shopper service, which wouldn't be worth it if you were just browsing on spec but if you knew you had to commit to buying an outfit for a big event it could save you a lot of time and dithering.

If, at the end of this list, you are more confused than ever, then I highly recommend you book yourself a personal style consultation. This is similar to a colour consultation but the professional's job is to take you through your unique proportions ("long back, short arms, small head", or whatever) and help you to know what shapes and styles suit you. (See the resources list for suggestions.) Once you know this information, it isn't going to be impossible for you to follow a fashion trend if you want to, but you will know how you can wear that trend, and if you can't, how you might be able to adapt it to suit you. Having an inner certainty that what you are wearing looks good on you will more than double your confidence.

There are lots of reasons why some of us have a complicated relationship with clothes. One is that it all seems so very complex and we are afraid of getting it wrong, so we stick to the safe and familiar, which is sometimes the same look we've worn since our teens. Another thing that puts some of us off is the whole idea of fashion and trends. Catwalks and fashion magazines are a world away from how we are living our lives; they seem elitist, expensive or simply bizarre. So, unless you are young, single and earning a lot of money, the idea of being a "slave to fashion" probably seems unappealing, expensive or faintly ridiculous. But on the other hand, no one wants to look completely out of date, so we keep a sneaky eye on what's in the magazines and on the rails.

The next problem with fashion is that we don't want to be pigeonholed yet we are aware that people might make assumptions about us based on what we are wearing. My clothing choices might land me unawares in a subset of society I know nothing about. I don't wish to be defined as "emo", "goth", "chav", "indie" or as "glam", "sloane", "mumsy" or "classic". When I get up in the morning I think I'm choosing items of clothing, not badges of belonging. I'm putting on trousers or a skirt, not a personality. I have a personality; the trick with clever dressing is to know how to express that personality. When you match your inner person with your outer look, you will feel much more at ease with yourself. The "real me" is the person inside, but for some, the clothing on the outside is the means for establishing an identity. Not that it's always a bad thing for clothing to create your identity; if you wear a uniform as a nurse or a doctor, your clothes are performing a useful function, sending out a short-hand message about who you are and the authority you have to do what you are doing.

Clothes speak volumes. They reveal information about us. They can help us feel more confident and inspire others to have confidence in us. Certain clothes are simply appropriate or not appropriate for certain situations, and all you need is an awareness of your surroundings to tell you that. I wouldn't wear a low-scoop neck line to work in an all-male prison – that's a no-brainer! – but then, I wouldn't wear one anyway, due to lack of boobs! But I do realize that I use clothes to give me power. When I used to work in a school I was aware that I always wore a certain blue jacket on days that I knew would be challenging. Putting on that particular well-tailored jacket somehow made me feel more in control. I didn't think anyone else ever noticed, but it was a fourteen-year-old girl who said to me, "I knew you meant business today, Miss – you had your blue jacket on." She was a perceptive kid! Clothes can indeed confer power. When you feel good in what you are wearing, you can walk into a room with poise and confidence. You can also relax and forget yourself more easily, rather than feeling hampered by self-consciousness. Lipstick has the same magic effect. A little bit of lippy can have a magical effect before a scary moment.

Using clothing and make-up as a "prop" in this way is yet another thing

"I think we could look at a bright belt to show off that
slim figure"

"Certain clothes are simply appropriate." (p.139)

that makes some people feel uncomfortable, like they are putting on an act. I don't see it that way. My motive is not to impress, compete or manipulate. Instead, like those Danish and Russian women we mentioned earlier, I dress up because it's fun. It's something I do for myself. Clothes and make-up are just tools that help me be the best that I can be. When I get it right, then what I'm wearing helps me to do whatever it is I'm doing; it doesn't detract or get in the way. If I'm well dressed and comfortable with my "look", it's easier to forget about myself, which frees me to be more aware of others. Clothing needs to be used out of a sense of self-worth and self-belief that is firmly rooted. As Mike Starkey puts it very succinctly: "Style is a gift for a secure identity, not a substitute for a lost identity."[1]

It might seem odd to have such a long section on clothes in a book with this title, but by now I hope you've realized that this isn't a book about actually being naked, but about feeling good about yourself and thoroughly at home with the body you have. Changing the way you think about yourself is essential to reaching a place of contentment and self-acceptance, and some people manage to think positively by giving themselves a lot of up-beat pep talks. Nothing wrong with that, but I would suggest that it's your underlying beliefs that inform your thought life. If you believe, "I'm worth it, I'm special, I'm unique, I'm loved, I'm treasured", then you will dress, live and act in a way that expresses that self-confidence. Do those phrases sound arrogant? Far-fetched? Narcissistic? They are merely a shorter version of all the beliefs I told you about at the start of Chapter 2. They are what God says about me. These are the foundations for my self-belief. He doesn't call me "rubbish" so I should not see myself that way. If you are hiding in your clothes, if you feel that make-up is your mask, if you feel that there is a huge distance between how you really feel and what you look like, then the next chapter is for you.

If, on the other hand, you do have at least a little self-belief, then I'd encourage you to step bravely into your wardrobe, throw out everything you haven't worn for the last year and take a good look at what's left. Is it working for you? Is it purely functional? Why? What does it say about you? What message would you like to get out there? Have a friend round to help with the clear out. Have a clothes swap party – very popular in these frugal times – but most of all, have fun with clothes.

Make-up

If you've been paying attention as we've gone along you'll already know that I grew up in a church community that was fairly disapproving of self-enhancement, and I currently have just ten items in my make-up bag, so you may feel I'm hardly the person to be telling you about make-up! But all ten items work well for me and, from my experience, I can at least tell you that what you don't know about make-up you can learn and that the whole business isn't as complicated, mysterious or expensive as the cosmetics industry would have us believe. I also know that make-up is fun, makes you look great and can work very well without being at all obvious.

So what's in my kit?

Foundation

This is the single most important ingredient, and it's worth taking time and spending a bit of money to get it right. Go to the make-up counter of a big department store and make a nuisance of yourself. You need to find a shade that disappears into your skin, which feels curiously like buying something you can't see, but it works. Foundation evens out your skin tone and covers small blemishes. If you're not convinced, try putting it on half your face and then see the difference. You can dot it on with your fingertips or use a make-up sponge, but less is more and don't forget to blend it down your neck. The worst mistake is to slap it on like a cake and stop at your jaw line. There are so many products out there, I couldn't possibly give any general advice except to say that if you are younger and still suffering with spots, you might want to go for an oil-free foundation.

Concealer

The second most important item should be a shade lighter than your foundation and go on before your foundation. It should lessen dark rings under the eyes and can be used elsewhere to cover blemishes – for example, around the nose. Dab it or tap it to blend it into the under-eye area; never rub in the under-eye area where the skin is very delicate.

Blusher powder

Powder blusher will stay on longer but if you have a mature, creased face, cream blusher will look more natural. Blusher goes on the apples of your cheeks; grin madly into the mirror if you can't find them! The most common mistake with blusher is the tramline effect of two solid lines down your cheekbones. The right tool for the task – a big rounded blusher brush – will help you get a softer effect.

Lipstick

The colour is clearly the most important factor in getting the right lipstick. I can't possibly advise you; you need to experiment. If the colour is too strong, all that people will notice is the lipstick. You want a colour that enhances and doesn't "shout". Winters can "shout" so long as they have a dramatic personality. Remember that darker colours can be quite ageing, so if you are a mature lady and you haven't changed your colour in years, you might want to go up a shade or two. Once you find a colour you like, buy at least two so you have one with you and one at home. The worst mistake with lips is using a lip liner that's darker than your lipstick, and once the lippy has worn off all you are left with is a rather odd drawn-on outline. It may never have occurred to you to use a lip liner anyway. That's fine; why add another product unnecessarily? If you want something in addition to lipstick that's easily applied and portable, gloss would be a better bet, as a quick re-apply should refresh what's already there.

Eyeshadow

Here's the bit that flummoxes a lot of us. My best advice on colour and how to apply it is "Get some professional advice." Basically, light shades lift or open the eyelid and dark shades draw down. It's best to use a highlighter over the lid with a darker shade, applied as wedge/triangle in the outer corner to add definition. Again you can get books on the subject but you can also pay for a make-up lesson in most beauty therapy shops. In my experience this was another really worthwhile investment. Come to think of it, I only invested my time. My mother paid, God bless her. What a lovely gift to give to someone – you just need to get the gift tag right. "You look awful, here's a make-up lesson" probably wouldn't be so helpful as "To help your inner beauty shine out…"

Eyeliner

This bit of kit makes eyes stand out as much as or even more than mascara. You don't need to apply it around the whole eyelid; along the lower lid from the outside to the halfway point will do the trick. Blend it and smudge it. Pencils often have sponge tip at the opposite end to help with this. You are not trying for a solid black line. I use a powder and a narrow eyeliner brush; it goes on a little easier than a pencil, especially if you're short-sighted or have shaky hands.

Mascara

You are looking for something that goes on easily without clogging and comes off easily too without tugging. Mind you, if you are prone to emotion, you don't want it to come off that easily either. You can get waterproof/sensitive/good-for-contact-lens-wearers mascara as well as different colours. You need to shop around. If you really hate putting on mascara then you might like to think about having your lashes dyed. This only takes about twenty minutes and is a fun, cheaper treatment with quite a high impact. For example, if you were going away on holiday and were going to be in and out the swimming pool, this would be a good alternative. One other thing about mascaras: of all the things in your make-up bag, they have a use-by date. Chuck them out if you've had them for more than six months. At least this will act as an incentive to use them regularly.

So those are the seven things in my kit. Yes, I know I said "ten" – the other three items are tools: a blusher brush, an eyeliner brush and an eyeshadow brush. I'm aware that this is really minimalist and if you really know about make-up you're probably shouting now about all sorts of other items you could add. What about face powder? Yes, this is very good for fixing your foundation. What about eyebrow pencils? Apparently they are great if you have scrawny eyebrows, but that's definitely not my problem. I did warn you this would be very biased and subjective. But ignorance is not the reason I haven't made this section more complicated. I'm trying to appeal to the woman who wears little or no make-up because she feels it's far too complicated and she's afraid of getting it wrong. It isn't that hard and it doesn't need to be that expensive either. Just go and have fun!

Hair

It's a rare woman who can feel good in her body if her hair is a mess. As your "crowning glory", taking care of your hair and thinking carefully about style and colour will pay big dividends in terms of your overall look. Younger women can get away with just about anything in terms of style or colour, although obviously certain styles will look better on certain face shapes. Older women are a bit more limited. Long hair is very ageing on an older woman; it can also get scraggly and wiry as it's just not in the same condition it was when you had long flowing locks in your teens. Get it cut! Even if your husband nurses fond fantasies about long hair, tell him to get over it! If you can tolerate a bob style, the ideal length for an older woman is above her shoulders but below her jaw; this gives movement and softness around her face and can cover droopy jowls. If like me, you need it shorter because you don't have the time or patience for daily styling, you should put some shape and softness into your style with layers, and don't go too short. Only those with a very fine bone structure on an elfin face and with excellent skin can look good with very short hair.

As for colour, you need to make your own mind up about going grey or covering up. I don't mind what you do, just don't make anyone feel they should do the same as you. Personally I think colour is fun and grey is ageing, unless you go that beautiful slate grey or pure white. As you get older one solid block of colour on your head is ageing, so you'd be better to think about highlights or lowlights, depending on your skin tone. None of this is cheap. Hair is the one area that defines me as high maintenance – colouring, cutting it or getting rid of it. Which brings us on to:

Beauty treatments

The things you do daily and the things you eat will have more effect on your skin than treatments you pay for. So moisturize twice daily (it doesn't have to be fancy or expensive stuff), eat fruit and vegetables and drink lots of water.

I'm not a masochist but I only ever seem to go to salons for painful treatments. I've rarely felt able to justify the expense on pedicures, manicures, facials or body wraps, no matter how lovely they all sound, but they do make great gifts (hint, hint!). When I'm paying I want a treatment that makes an instant visible difference, so in my case this always involves hair. I have experienced all known forms of hair removal: waxing, sugaring, threading, electrolysis (sticking a needle down every follicle and zapping the hair at its root – you don't hear much about this now). If laser hair removal had been invented when I was younger, I would have tried that too, as that's the one thing I haven't had done. My favourite treatments used to be any of the above, mostly on my legs, but I also used to go for eyebrow shaping and upper-lip waxing. However, I've now learnt to do these last two for myself. Tidy, well-shaped eyebrows can be as dramatic as a facelift; if you've never had your eyebrows shaped, you'd be amazed at the effect. If you have anything more than soft down on your upper lip, don't bother bleaching it; this will only make it more obvious against a dark skin tone (and if you have upper lip hair you are likely to have darker skin tone). Just whip it off with some facial wax strips. These are really cheap now and yes, the hair will grow back, but not any worse than before, and it's an easily repeated process.

I have a favourite birthday card pinned on my board. It's a middle-aged woman peering into a mirror and the caption reads: "Phew! Another birthday and still no beard!" If I were on a desert island my luxury would be a pair of eyebrow tweezers. The reason I own so many pairs is because if I forget to take a pair with me when I go away, I have to buy a new one. If I don't always forget, because I'm so attached to them, the other mistake is to leave them in my hand luggage, so I've also left a fair few pairs at airports around the world.

Other people would have other essentials they couldn't do without: hand cream, body moisturizer and lip salve would all fight for second place on my list behind the tweezers. And other people have favourite treatments that for them feel essential. A massage can be powerfully therapeutic and a great way to de-stress. A new set of nails can be a great pick-me-up. A facial or a series of facials can do wonders for problematic skin. As I said before, I can't advise you about what works and doesn't work for you. I can tell you, if it helps, that there is a great biblical precedent for beauty treatments. Esther spent a whole year pampering herself before she was presented to the King, and the lover in the Song of Solomon doesn't seem to have cheapskated on spices and perfumes. You are the only person who can work out what works for you and what's worth the money. I'd advise you not be dazzled by fancy packaging and obscure ingredients. If you are looking for a moisturizer you can buy peptides,

"Goose grease was all WE could get when we were gels"

"Fancy packaging and obscure ingredients" (p.146)

retinoids or even something containing the fermented extract of a kombucha mushroom (I kid you not), but you'll pay for it, and paying a large sum for a product doesn't necessarily guarantee it will work any better than a cheaper alternative. It's the habit of cleansing and moisturizing that will make more difference than the product.

Then finally there is the more extreme end of beauty treatments: peels, botox, liposuction and surgery. I think you need to think very carefully and do a lot of research before you decide to go for anything that carries a risk. In the UK there are still no regulations that apply to cosmetic filler-type injections. Basically anyone can inject them, and although beauty therapists can be trained to inject them, they are not medical professionals and these are not classed as prescription drugs. You need look hard at the possibility of it all going wrong. What redress would you have? Signing a consent form is more often a let-out clause for the practitioner. My feeling is that there are cases where cosmetic surgery is justified – for example, in a case of extreme scarring. I also think breast reduction can make life a lot more bearable for someone with very large breasts which can put a huge strain on your neck, back and shoulders. But all of these decisions are highly individual. I wouldn't dream of saying you should do this or you should never to this. I would just have you ask yourself some searching questions:

- Is my view about this feature likely to change as I grow older? Am I taking a long-term view?
- If I sort out this problem, will there just be something else that bothers me?
- Are there other, less risky ways to deal with the problem, such as diet and exercise?
- What is it that's making me feel so bad about the feature I want to change? Am I trying to live up to an unrealistic media ideal? Have I never dealt with negative messages from my childhood or from bullies? Might there be a way of addressing the feelings first which would make the surgery unnecessary?

"P" is for Presentation: the final factor in a trio of things we can do for ourselves that will make a big difference to how we feel about our bodies. Easier than exercise and more fun than dieting, self-enhancement is a popular route to self-confidence. Transformation is possible, even on a budget. We run two risks: either we won't attempt it because we don't think we're worth it. Or, looking better than we feel, we will become aware of a gap between how we look and who we really are. We need to learn to love our bodies, but to do that we need to learn to be loved. It's to these inner struggles we now turn our attention.

NOTES

1.Mike Starkey, *Fashion and Style*, Crowborough: Monarch, 1995.

Chapter 8

Sham, Shame and Self-Destruction

Now that we have covered the big three areas for self-improvement – diet, exercise and personal grooming – I'm guessing there will be a significant proportion of readers who are left thinking, "Yes, but…" More accurately, that should read, "Yes, butt…" because what they are actually thinking is, "Yes, but you haven't seen the size of *my* butt" or "You have no idea how many diets *I've* tried and failed" or "You can't possibly expect me to feel positive about *this* body: these lumpy thighs, these flabby arms, this enormous belly, these short, fat legs, this face, these hands…" and so on and so on.

Well, yes, I do, actually. It was my clearly stated aim at the outset that I want every reader to feel positive about the body they have, even the way that body is right now. How could I have had such an ambitious aim? I'm not naïve enough to think that the surface rearrangements I've been suggesting for the last three chapters will make all the difference. They will help. In fact they will help enormously. Why else would I have taken the time to persuade you to improve your diet, take up exercise and revamp your wardrobe? In fact, I'd be bold enough to say that if you were to follow my advice to the letter, you would be transformed. And if that happens for you, wonderful! Please send me the "before" and "after" photos!

But I am not under any illusions about how thoroughly you will take my advice. I also know how hard it can be to make some of those changes in lifestyle. When it comes to finding reasons why the diet plan or the exercise programme "would never work for me", I've been at the top of the class. Stop and remind yourself of the various points so far in this book where you have thought or said, "That's all very well, but…" and you'll realize you may not be very far behind me.

Let's be honest here: I don't take all my own advice. I'm not some health and fitness guru, and my daughter just about fell over laughing when I told her I'd written a section on make-up. I may have recommended exercise on five days a week, but I only manage about three sessions a week myself. I know it's the right advice to tell you to "eat when you're hungry and stop when you are full", but, just like anyone else, I sometimes eat when I'm bored and stop when I'm stuffed. Are you disappointed in me? Have I undermined my own best efforts to help you towards a "new transformed you"? Why am I being so honest?

Because I don't want you to believe the lie; not a lie about me – after all, I have tried to represent myself honestly. I mean THE lie. The lie that says, *"If only I could get everything sorted – my weight down, my appetite under control, my body toned, my style perfected – then I'll be happy, then I'll be content, then I'll love the body I've got."* This is THE big lie and I don't want you to fall for it. This lie is not true because (a) you won't ever get everything sorted anyway: you can tone your upper arms till kingdom come, but your boobs will still eventually succumb to gravity. And (b) even if you could sort out everything on the surface and succeed in looking good all the time, keeping that show on the road is a full-time operation. If feeling good depends on having your roots tinted, your eyebrows tidied, your legs waxed and everything between your armpits and thighs held in place by reinforced elastic, then I hate to break it to you, honey, but there is going to come a day when it all hangs out!

The lie says, "Everything depends on how I look." The truth is, "It's all a matter of how you feel", and if you feel good about yourself, then you can still actually feel good even on a day when you don't look so great. My ambition has been to help you get to such a place. Maybe as you've been reading you have actually changed something about your lifestyle or appearance, and that's fine, but I will only have truly succeeded if I have helped you change the way you feel.

My aim has been for you to allow yourself to feel good about your body. I want you to be able to say, "I am an amazing person and I have an amazing body. It is the only body I'll ever have, so while there may be things that are less than ideal about this body, I am going to celebrate it and love it and do my best to look after it." This is the attitude that says, "I have a belly, so let's learn to belly dance" rather than "I have a belly; find me some place to hide".

I saw a programme on TV recently about women who feel so bad about their post-pregnancy shape that they sign up for a "mummy makeover". They pay $20,000 for a three-in-one package of surgery: a breast lift, a tummy tuck and liposuction, entailing eight hours in the theatre. The husband of a woman undergoing this procedure comments (in a way that he thinks is supportive): "You can have everything in the world but if you're not happy with yourself, it's not worth anything." Without a shade of self-awareness, he expresses a profound truth whilst totally missing the point. How does he know that his wife will finally be happy with herself when everything's been surgically enhanced? How can she know that? She's been made to believe the lie, that if only she can control her body and look good, then she'll be truly happy and content. The chances are, the outcome won't live up to the perfection she desired. The scars will distress her or even if she's pleased with the result, some other body part or life issue will become the focus of her concern. She has to learn to be happy with herself first and if she does that, she'll probably save herself $20,000. It might also be worth stopping for a moment and thinking what message does all this misery over her body give to the child whose arrival "messed up" mummy's body and caused her to be so unhappy?

The problem is in her head. The problem is not in her body. This woman has believed the lie. We prefer to think that our problem is only "skin deep" (OK, maybe as deep as the layer of fat beneath the skin) because then it will only take some surface rearrangements to make us happy. We have to actually own up and admit the problem is much deeper. The issue of self-loathing begins in our heads and hearts. It's all about how we think and how we feel and how we talk to ourselves. It's very little about how we actually look.

If I'd had the time I could have written at least three more chapters' worth of tips and techniques that would help you look after your body and dress to impress. There's no end of good advice out there, all promising to transform your life and make you "feel" good, but as I hinted at the outset, feelings that only flow one way (I look good therefore I feel good) are not very stable. As soon as I stop looking good, I stop feeling good. Now, I haven't wanted to deny that looking good will go a long way towards making you feel good; in fact I've actively encouraged you to look as good as you can, but I would have sold you short if I tried to make out that was all there was to it; I might even have helped you believe the lie. I've had a bigger aim. My hope is that you can find a better reason for a positive self-belief that will shine out, whatever you look like.

There is a saying: "Perfect is the enemy of good." If you remember, we started this book with the concept of perfection and we thought about the effect of all those images of female perfection that bombard us daily. We reflected on the fact that even celebrities with huge budgets to help them look good can still have their imperfections commented on viciously by the press. But even their shortcomings don't comfort us; they merely raise the bar of "perfection" higher still. In all this maelstrom of expectation, we have been losing our sense of perspective, our balance and our ability to say, "Actually, I'm good enough." Learning to love your body is about saying exactly that. "I'm good enough" is the first phrase I'd like you to put in your self-talk phrase book. We have to find replacements and alternatives for some of the negative things we say about ourselves, either out loud or in our head. Negative self-talk has a great deal of power. It doesn't just make us feel bad, it actually affects the way we behave and the choices we make.

In the second chapter I recommended four "antidote attitudes", one of which was "be content". Being content is the "good enough" attitude I want to help you develop in relation to your body. The stakes are high. Developing this attitude is not some kind of spiritual add-on that will enhance your life. It's far more important than that. I would call it a survival strategy. If you try to live life without learning contentment, you could end up in one of three desperate places: sham, shame or self-destruction.

Sham

Sham is when you actually look great on the outside but feel rubbish inside. You are probably the envy of your friends. You dress well, exercise regularly or are simply naturally slim. You've either had an unfair share of genetic goodies from the good-looking department or have a big enough bank account to fund any form of self-enhancement you desire. Everyone thinks that you've got it all together because you look like you have. You'd hate for anyone to know "the real you": your fears, your obsessions, your self-doubt. Perhaps there are hurts that you've carried for years and "looking good" is part of your armour. You're never going to let anyone hurt you again. You're not going to appear vulnerable and you don't want anyone to know how deeply committed you are to managing the way people react to you, what they think and believe about you. Your "face in the jar by the door" is there to ensure no one sees the real you.

Not every good-looking woman is living this lie, even if envious onlookers might prefer to think so. So if you do come into this category, you will probably be the only person who will know. If there is a constant gap between how you feel and how you look, and you know that looking good matters hugely to you, then the chances are you might be living a sham. Most of us occasionally feel worse than we look and use make-up and power-dressing to bolster our feelings of inadequacy, especially in scary situations. But if you always feel this way this is a cause for concern. Your only route out of this situation is to learn contentment, to come to terms with the parts of your personality that you'd rather hide and to find someone who knows you "warts and all" and yet still loves you.

Shame

Shame is sometimes hidden behind the sham but often it's more obvious, especially in our body language. Shame is when every encounter with your physical self is a cause of self-recrimination, disgust or embarrassment. It might be when you are in front of a mirror, or when you shop for clothes, when you find yourself out of breath at the top of stairs, when you refuse to take your child swimming for fear of everyone looking at you, or when you go out for a meal and you think everyone's talking about what you're eating.

Shame is most in evidence by the stream of negative things we say to ourselves: "I'm such a pig, I'm ugly, huge, gross, repulsive, manly, disgusting, I look like a freak, I have no self-control." Shame is the feeling that we have failed in some way, that there is a standard we haven't met. We might feel we fall short, there is some way in which we are inadequate: not clever, not witty, not articulate, not competent, not beautiful, not accepted. Or we might feel we are too much: too needy, too sensitive, too emotional, too anxious or too damaged for any one person to cope with. Shame is the feeling that we are to blame, that somehow it's all our own fault.

Most of us have lost the ability to trace the source of all this negative self-talk. It's just so persistent, we don't question it. In Chapter 3 I tried to encourage you to think about the experiences that may have left you feeling rejected as a child. Maybe you weren't girly enough, maybe you weren't bright enough, maybe you were "too demanding", or you were told you were "that kind of girl" and had it coming to you. The experience of rejection can range from simply not being fully accepted for who you were (I say "simply" only because it's a common experience, not because it's slight in its effect) all the way to being emotionally, physically or sexually abused. Disgust and self-loathing are not uniquely linked to sexual abuse, but overcoming these strong forms of shame will be essential in the recovery of anyone who has been so abused. "Recovery" might even seem too unlikely a word to use; perhaps "a route forward" might seem more achievable? One strategy for finding your route forward would be to challenge the negative self-talk and replace it with more positive statements (more on this later). But the key resource for moving on from a crippling sense of shame is to find someone who knows you warts and all and genuinely loves you anyway.

Self-destruction

Self-destruction is a destination. It's the place you might end up if you don't address the issue of sham or shame. Self-destruction covers the full range of behaviours, from compulsive shopping, binge drinking, risky sex and drug abuse (all of which appear to be more in our control) to eating disorders, such as anorexia or bulimia, including forms of self-harm (where we appear to be controlled by a mental illness or compulsion). No one with healthy self-esteem, no one who believes they have value, no one who has developed an ounce of resilience, will choose to self-destruct. But it doesn't take much to deprive us of those factors that protect us. It could be a set of circumstances which make us feel isolated, a negative remark we take to heart, a rejection such as a relationship breakup, being made redundant or a long-term stress that grinds us down. If we use the analogy of a car which has a fuel tank, you have two fuel tanks: an emotional tank and a physical one. Your food supplies your physical energy but self-esteem and resilience are the essential additives you need in your emotional tank.

Resilience is the inner quality that can accept that not everything goes well all the time: there will be bad days, good days and in-between days. Resilient people can have bad stuff happen to them without them assuming it's their fault and without them losing hope that a better time will come eventually. Resilience is a very important quality. Combine it with a bit of self-belief and perspective, and you have an outlook that will help you face most crises without falling apart or resorting to self-destruction. The problem is that resilience and self-esteem seem to be in short supply.

More and more people who experience emotional distress do not have the resources to cope and turn instead to addictive behaviours or self-destructive strategies. There are so many different reasons why people end up in a pattern of self-destructive behaviour, it would be a terrible over-simplification to say it was all down to one or another factor, but there is one way forward that is valid for everyone in a spiral of self-destruction: finding someone who knows them warts and all and still loves them.

You may have noticed by now that I've given the same solution to all three issues: to find someone who knows you warts and all and still loves you. It sounds like a hopelessly romantic notion. How do you find this person? What if it doesn't work out? What if they reject you? Doesn't that leave you more screwed up than ever? If you are single, divorced or have just been dumped, I wouldn't have blamed you for shouting at my suggestion. On the off chance you haven't thrown the book away, I'd like to clarify! I'm *not* talking about a romantic attachment.

If you are Christian you are possibly waiting for me to spiritualize this suggestion and tell you that God is the person who knows you warts and all and yet still loves you completely. Because I believe that's true and also because I believe there are sound reasons for recommending a relationship with God, I won't disappoint you but I will make you wait just a little longer. I'm going to come to the connection between God and self-esteem in the final chapter.

I know that the idea of a relationship with God can be a difficult solution to hear, either because you're not sure if he's there, or you don't like what you've heard about him, or you think he was part of your original problem. So I want to spend this chapter honouring the more human solutions first: the power of friends, sisters, brothers, mothers, fathers, counsellors, colleagues and fellow human beings in general. Don't let's underestimate the effect that ordinary human relationships can have in our lives. It would be unrealistic to ignore the fact that most of us, for most of the time, rely on other people to help us feel good about ourselves. Positive feedback, attention, affection, appreciation, sharing experiences and discussing life in general – these are the ways we gauge who we are, how we are perceived and whether we matter. It would be very odd if this weren't the case, even though we all know it's not helpful to become too dependent on approval from other people. Ordinary human relationships are the way most of us find acceptance, love and the courage to face our fears.

If you have recognized that your self-loathing is a result of sham or shame and if you want to be free from a self-destructive addiction or illness, then it is highly likely that it will be a human being or a group of human beings who will help you find a way forward. They may or may not help you towards a relationship with God. The first time many of us met God, we met him in other people, so I hope you'll consider the reasons I give for not ruling him out, but I accept that the most easily accessible form of love and acceptance that we experience comes from other human beings. They might be professionals such as counsellors or psychiatrists or they may simply be faithful friends with ears to listen and patience to accept you as you are. If they have no agenda to sort you out but only an agenda to love you, so much the better. A combination of friends and professional help is ideal. The love of a life partner such as a husband or a wife can be hugely powerful in restoring our sense of self-belief. Such are hard to find and worth their weight in gold.

Because some of these sources of informal support are risky, I'd encourage you to also seek professional help. By "risky" I mean that not everyone finds a loving life partner and even if they do, expecting someone else to be "everything" for you can place too great a strain on a relationship. Friends can also be fallible. They sometimes say well-meaning but stupid things and they are not always there for us when we need them to be. People, even those who matter to us, have other priorities – their work, their own families, their own problems. They may move on or move away. For these reasons I think you shouldn't undervalue professional help. I'm not promising that a counsellor is immune from saying unhelpful things, but a good counsellor will have safe boundaries (i.e. he or she will ensure they won't be overwhelmed by your problem), appropriate training and experience, and will offer you support without any expectation that you will care for them in return. Unlike friends and family, the expectations and agenda are very clear.

Up until now I've been talking as if you are the one with a body-image problem. But I'm very aware that you may in fact have no body-image issues of your own, but you have picked this book up because you are bewildered by the behaviour of someone you love: a daughter, a niece, a close friend who seems to have pressed the self-destruct button so regularly, you wonder where it will all end and how you can possibly help them. For the next part of this chapter I want to spend some time unpacking some of the more common self-destructive issues. I hope the strategies and information I offer will be useful to care-givers, those people who stand by and feel helpless or despairing. There *are* things that you can do that will make a difference.

Even though all human relationships are fallible, I do believe that all of us have the capacity to offer respect, acceptance, dignity and love to someone else in a way that can powerfully affect their life. If this were not true, then all the humanitarian work around the world might as well end right now. When I put it like that, it sounds obvious that we can make a difference to other people, but when it's your daughter who is not eating or your friend who is binge drinking or your partner who self-harms, it's likely that you will feel utterly inadequate and totally overwhelmed by the scale of the problem. You might feel frightened that it's somehow your fault, or you worry that you might make it worse. Sometimes we are so afraid of getting it wrong; we don't know where to start or what response to make so we are tempted to back away. Please don't do that for the person you love.

If on the other hand, you are the one with a body-image issue and it has led you to one or more of these self-destructive forms of behaviour, then I hope you can "see yourself" in the descriptions below. You can apply the strategies to your own life if that seems helpful, but I'd encourage you above all else to own up to the fact that you are struggling with one of these issues. This almost certainly means talking to someone about it: a GP, a helpline, a friend or whoever you feel could safely handle that information. If you are worried they might feel overwhelmed by your revelation, loan them this book. After all, I'm about to give them a load of suggestions about how to love and support you! If naming the problem out loud is just too hard, you could just put a note in the relevant page saying "this is me".

Eating disorders

Anorexia, Bulimia and Chaotic or Compulsive Eating are all uppermost in our minds when we think about the self-destructive behaviours linked to body image. It isn't always body image that is the trigger factor but an eating disorder usually starts when someone who is already struggling with other things in life decides that everything would be better if only they were thinner. Sometimes an eating disorder develops when someone discovers they are "good" at dieting. They succeed in losing weight and this brings them some positive feedback from their friends. Their confidence goes up and suddenly being a success is pinned to being thin. Over 70 per cent of eating disorder sufferers say the first step in their disorder was dieting. Be very wary of young teenagers wanting to diet. A 10–14 year old should usually be gaining weight, not losing it, but with the rise in childhood obesity it's not possible to say categorically that children in this age group should never diet. However, a weight-loss programme for a child or young teenager ought to be medically supervised.

A diet doesn't always lead to an eating disorder but should always be approached with care. At any one time 50 per cent of teenage girls are on a diet and some studies have shown that up to 25 per cent of 11–14 year-old girls are struggling with an eating disorder. So not everyone who goes on a diet ends up with an eating disorder, nor is it just teenage girls who suffer; men, older women and children can all develop a disorder. Statistically though, children and teenagers are the most at risk. Under the age of eighteen, eating disorders cause more deaths than any other psychiatric illness, but full recovery is possible and early intervention has been shown to shorten the duration of the illness.[1]

There are several "personality" factors which will place a young person at higher risk of an eating disorder. Note that many of them are positive attributes, so mental illness is not the preserve of those we might judge to be weak. Someone is more susceptible if they are sensitive, self-critical, shy, inhibited, anxious, conscientious, hard-working, perfectionist, well behaved, highly motivated, determined and obsessive. The anorexic will often be the type of person who would support lots of other people and be the one not wanting to be a bother to anyone else. He or she will take life personally and seriously. They are likely to feel uncomfortable with negative feelings, not knowing how to handle neediness, anger or frustration, so they hold these feelings at bay. Anorexia is a way of numbing the feelings.

The personality of a bulimia sufferer may be quite different in that they will outwardly appear confident and outgoing. They are often socially competent; they may well be quite impulsive. Underneath the sunny outlook they are full of doubts and inadequacies. They will hide these feelings; they hide food and they hide the fact that they are bingeing and vomiting. Overall people with bulimia stay at near-normal weight, making this condition much harder to spot. Over time there will eventually be some physical symptoms due to the fact that repeated vomiting will damage their teeth and saliva glands, but this will be some time after the psychological damage and shame of this cycle of bingeing and vomiting has set in. If your daughter is going to the bathroom promptly after meal times, maybe playing the radio loudly and then flushing the toilet several times, it may well be a good idea to gently raise a concern with her. (I'm going to use the mother/daughter situation as an example, partly because it is a common scenario, but I don't mean to imply it is the only example. It could be a housemate you are concerned for or a work colleague, and they may be male.)

Saying nothing and doing nothing in the hope that "she'll get over it" or "it's just a phase" is almost always the wrong course of action, but reacting in a panic, coming down on her angrily, shouting, yelling or making threats, is not the way to raise the concern either. If you suspect a problem, wait till you've processed the possibility, perhaps even talked to a confidential helpline. Then at a time you both feel calm, talk about how she is feeling at the moment, try to keep the focus on feelings rather than food, but not to such an extent that you don't actually mention your concerns over food.

It may be that you are not the best person to talk to her. If you're too likely to get upset and angry or if you just think she'd be more likely to listen to someone else, then stand aside, but be aware that she may resent you for involving someone else and discussing your concerns with them. You need to balance your need to talk with her need for confidentiality and respect, so only talk to people you trust. If you are not the best person, you can still try to ensure she or he talks to someone: a friend, a youth group leader, a teacher or a GP.

You can visit your GP on behalf of your child under eighteen. This can be a very helpful first step but it's best to let your child know that you are going to do that and encourage them to come with you if they feel they can. If they don't want to come, go anyway and keep them informed about the conversation. Obviously, if you are not the person's parent or if your child is over eighteen, this option is not open to you. All you can do is encourage her to go.

If you're really not sure whether you are worrying unnecessarily and don't want to risk saying something out of turn, then the following signs ought to ring alarm bells: if the person is known to be experiencing emotional stress but he or she clams up over feelings; a sudden disproportionate concern about weight and appearance; becoming overly critical and perfectionist; being irritable and inflexible (tricky, as this describes most teenagers); any rigid dieting behaviour that is very limited or restricted, especially when previously favourite foods become "forbidden"; an unwillingness to participate in social eating; avoidance of mealtimes or excuses for not eating; excessive exercise and sudden enthusiasm to cook "treats" such as cakes and biscuits for everyone else to enjoy (this last one is a demonstration of self-control).

The type of symptoms experienced by an anorexic will obviously be weight loss in the first instance. If the child is under ten this can become very serious very quickly, hence the need for a prompt response. For a girl beyond puberty one of the first symptoms will be that her periods will stop. A sufferer is likely to experience obsessive thought patterns, they may have difficulty communicating, they will have poor concentration and their short-term memory will be impaired. They will become isolated and withdrawn. As the illness progresses, they are at far greater risk of self-harm and suicide, they become sensitive to cold, suffer poor circulation and loss of muscle mass in essential organs such as the heart.

So what strategies can help if someone close to you has an eating disorder?

The first step towards recovery is acknowledging the issue, which is why I've encouraged you to talk to the person about your concerns, and unless your mind is completely put at rest by this conversation, follow it up with a visit to your GP. You can't, by sheer force of argument, bring someone to the point of admitting they have a problem. If they are determined to deny it you have to accept that, but at the very least you should not be drawn into a conspiracy of silence on the matter. If you love someone you will tell them when you are worried about them. If they won't listen you don't have a right to cross-examine, browbeat or hassle them over the issue on every occasion you see them. Instead you have to sit back, keep expressing love and wait. You can still give them plenty of time and opportunity to express their feelings. You need to create an atmosphere of acceptance where feelings are not bad or good, merely comfortable or uncomfortable. They need to know from you that it's OK to feel needy, it's normal to feel angry.

If the person has acknowledged the problem, remember that is only the first step. Don't expect recovery to be instant. If an eating disorder has really taken hold, you need to take the long view; try to keep a hopeful picture of recovery in your head but locate it someway in the future. An impatience for the sufferer to "get over it" will not help. He or she will have good days and they will have bad days. The recovery process will feel harder for the sufferer than being really ill; it will feel like a daily battle and it can be complete agony for the carer to observe. Someone with an eating disorder will almost certainly need professional support from doctors and/or psychiatrists and may need to be admitted to hospital. Contacting a support agency or charity can also be extremely helpful for both carer and sufferer (see the Resources section at the end of this book). Parents, particularly, need a safe place to download and sound off, as they will probably swing wildly from exasperation to desperation, feeling guilty, anxious and angry by turns. If you're going to have the capacity to love and affirm the sufferer in the middle of all those feelings, you definitely have to be talking to someone.

While no one would expect you to be a model of calm serenity, try if you can to take the emotion out of meal times and to try to show empathy with the sufferer, seeing things from their viewpoint. Feeling misunderstood will only make the person more likely to dig their heels in. Take the focus off food and try to keep it on feelings. This is the difference between "How are you feeling today?" and "What have you eaten today?" Even if a decision to change has been made, this will be a stop/start process and the individual will need a lot of love and affirmation. It's not a great idea to push for explanations over why she will eat this or that or how much she will eat. Give her the freedom to make some choices and express confidence in her ability to make responsible choices. If you are the parent of a sufferer and you have other children, it will be important to set boundaries about when or how you talk about the issue, otherwise it can come to dominate the whole family. This is very difficult to avoid, so don't assume other siblings are not affected by it.

Remember, you need to affirm the whole person, not just the body. If your life has become dominated by your body image, you need reminding that you are not just a body. You also have intelligence, understanding, friendships, inner qualities like beliefs, personality traits and preferences, skills, experiences and interests. If you can help the sufferer see herself in this wider way, then gradually life will fill with greater meaning and the underlying causes of the eating disorder will be resolved.

Another useful strategy is to help the sufferer externalize the eating disorder. You may be able to do this by calling "it" a bad voice or a goblin that causes negative thoughts. It's not that you are shifting the "blame" or sense of responsibility, but it's easier to fight an enemy on the outside rather than deal with a constant inner struggle. Personifying the compulsion as some exterior force can give the young person something to actively resist, maybe by making posters along the lines of "Don't give in to the goblin".[2]

If you are not caring for someone else trapped by an eating disorder – if in fact you realize that you are the one with food issues – then I hope you'll still be able to take something from all I have said, particularly about acknowledgment being the first step to recovery. If you are going to recover you're going to have to first decide you want to recover. Try to imagine what your life would be like if it weren't dominated by food. Be patient with yourself. You need to learn that having a day when you slip back into self-destructive ways does not wipe out all your progress so far, nor does it signal an inevitable slide downwards. Access all the help you can and if you can't talk about your feelings, at least keep a journal of them.

All of the strategies in the previous paragraphs could apply equally well to other forms of self-destructive, addictive behaviour. None of them represent an instant solution to the problem. They are very broad-brush principles about how to respond to someone behaving in a self-destructive way. It's important to keep in the forefront of your mind that a person who behaves this way is unhappy. Things are not going well for them. Sometimes their behaviours are dismissed as manipulative or attention seeking. This is not often the case. If a child is attention seeking by refusing to eat, then it follows that ignoring the behaviour would make them give up. If the behaviour persists, then continuing to ignore it is not going to suddenly make them change. Similarly, self-harm is usually a very secretive behaviour; the sufferer is not trying to manipulate a response from others. He or she is finding a way of releasing really bad feelings,

feelings that they haven't found any other safe way to express. Self-harm is a sign of distress. The person may feel so bad about themselves that they feel they deserve the pain; others speak about the temporary release of feeling that self-harm can give them. Self-injury can become a coping mechanism. Understanding why you feel the need to hurt yourself is crucial in finding a way forward from this kind of behaviour, so everything I've said about talking about feelings, accessing professional help or contacting specialist agencies applies. There are techniques and strategies that will help some people find less self-destructive ways to handle their feelings. Not all of them will help everybody. They might draw a picture of the wound they want to create and write or draw any associated feelings. Keep a journal of feelings. Talk to a friend or helpline when they feel a pressure to self-harm. Find other physical ways to get feelings out: punch or kick a cushion, shout, scream, cry or tear up an old telephone directory. Do something relaxing like having a bath or listening to music (self-harmers don't do self-care very easily so this suggestion won't work for everyone). Breathe slowly and deeply, think about breathing out anxiety and breathing in peace. Hold an ice-cube really tightly in the hand or flick an elastic band against the skin – both will hurt but they won't scar.[3]

Binge drinking and drug abuse are self-destructive behaviours that have been almost "normalized" by the society we live in. If we still hold to stereotypes in terms of who abuses drugs or alcohol, then we should abandon them. Studies have shown that it is the more educated women in their twenties who engage in binge drinking, to a greater extent than their less well-educated peers.[4] Likewise, drug abuse is not the preserve of those with limited life chances. It seems incredibly obvious and possibly simplistic, but at the root of all these issues are people who are unhappy, discontented for one reason or another, which just reinforces what I said earlier about contentment being a survival strategy for life.

So how do you generate this sense of contentment or self-belief? How can you go about raising a sense of self-confidence? What can you do to build up your own supply of resilience and self-esteem? Below is a list of things you can do for yourself or, if you are a parent, things you can do to build these qualities into your kids. Your mother was the first mirror you looked into to see what you were worth and your children are looking into you to assess their worth. As parents we have a huge responsibility, which is scary, but we also need to remember we have a great capacity to pour affirmation and unconditional love into someone we love.

- Be aware of what you child is reading and watching. It's unrealistic to say, "Don't look at women's magazines or watch makeover programmes", but at least discuss them with your daughter. Don't try to impose your views; just help her raise questions and think about the women represented as people, not mere bodies.
- Provide alternative reading material – for example, sports magazines with images of female athletes with powerful bodies. Talk about what they would need to eat to stay fit and healthy.
- Find some novels with strong female characters whose bodies are simply not the issue.
- Put up pictures on the fridge of normal or slightly heavier girls and add the slogan, "This is beautiful too".
- Give her information about how good nutrition will improve her skin, hair and overall development. She may moan, but she might read it.
- Embrace feelings: display a list of feelings words or little emoticons (simple round faces each showing a different emotion); try to encourage everyone in the family to use it from time to time, sometimes simply by pointing to the relevant feeling, even if they don't want to talk about it.
- Model the fact that you also experience negative feelings and demonstrate constructive ways of handling them – for example, "I need to be on my own for a bit because I'm feeling tired and irritable." Encourage them to express their feelings but don't insist that they talk to you. They could keep a private journal or talk to someone else.
- Help them to drop a perfectionist approach to life. Perfectionists will always feel guilty or feel like they have failed. "Good enough" will do just fine.
- Help them to become self-assertive. This will mean allowing them to take responsibility for certain tasks. We learn responsibility when we are trusted, even if we make mistakes. Resist the urge to step in and "fix" a problem for your teenager if you think they are capable

of resolving it for themselves. Sorting out issues and conflicts for themselves will give them the chance to develop valuable skills and experience.

- Help them to see themselves positively. Get everyone in the family to write down five or ten things they like about themselves.
- Challenge "self-talk" and be wary of "fat talk". "Self-talk" is all the negative things we say to ourselves such as: "I'm stupid/nobody likes me/I'll never succeed". "Fat talk" consists of all the ways in which we refer to food, weight or eating that load it with emotion and guilt; it includes nicknames that refer to food or weight (e.g. "porky", "fat face" or "pudding").
- Put positive "self-talk" statements on mirrors or on other obvious places around the house; for example: "I am one of a kind/I am loved/I am good at _____/Who I am is more important that what I look like/The best thing about _____ is _____/ If I do my best it doesn't matter whether or not I succeed." (I found my favourite of all these thoughts on a Post-it note. The first three versions of the first word are spelt wrong and scratched out: "Presistance, pesistance, presistence, persistence is way more important than perfection.")
- Challenge exaggerated thoughts and black-and-white thinking: "Being fat is the worst thing in the world" is an exaggeration. "Eating this chocolate will make me fat" is black-and-white thinking.
- Accept failure as a normal, even helpful part of life. A mistake or a dropped grade is not the end of the world.

Setting aside all the 101 ideas and strategies for helping someone overcome their difficulties, there are three fundamental attitudes you need to offer to anyone you love who is caught in a self-destructive cycle. The first is unconditional positive regard or "unconditional love". It's very important that they are accepted unconditionally. If your agenda is to "sort them out" you are not offering them what they need. You are responding to them simply in order to meet *your* need for them to get better. Say to yourself, "My only agenda is to love, it is not to solve, sort out, change or cajole this person. I need to love and accept them as they are." It can be very hard to resist the urge to "sort them out" – after all, their behaviour is harming them and exasperating you. But the fact is, you cannot "sort them out"; they have to take their own steps towards recovery, and all you can do is offer them love in the hope that it will provide them with the courage they need to move forward.

The second thing you offer is empathy: this means doing your very best to see things from their viewpoint, to understand the situation as they describe it, not as you experience it. This might mean accepting their version of events or at least their version of how those events affected them. Disagreeing with their point of view is more likely to back them into a corner; empathy is sitting in the corner with them and trying to feel what they feel.

The third thing you need to offer will probably sound unfamiliar: you need to offer "congruence". It's an odd kind of word that means you will do your best to offer consistency between what you say and how you feel. For example, if your overriding feeling towards them is that they are driving you bonkers, you should not lie and say, "I love you"; but neither would it help to tell them at that moment that "You're driving me bonkers"! Your responsibility in that situation is to take enough steps back from them and put enough safe boundaries in place so that you can recharge your own emotional tank, to give you the resources to cope. When you are sufficiently resourced, their behaviour won't necessarily change but you are in a better place, you are no longer exasperated, frustrated and tired, so you can then listen with love and patience. Looking after yourself in this way might seem an odd thing to offer someone else, but what you are offering them is the best of you. Congruence is almost impossible for a parent who is far too close to the situation to distance themselves from the pain it causes them. Parents need to offload their feelings of anger and sheer frustration with safe others. In practice "congruence" might mean not picking up the phone to your friend when you know you don't have the time or emotional capacity to listen with love and patience, but following up her call with a text arranging to see her another time. It's making sure your life is not dominated by someone else's problem, having enough space, peace and fun to recharge your own batteries.

Learning to love your body starts with changing how you think about yourself. It might then find expression in how you care for yourself in terms of diet, exercise and grooming. At some point along the way you have to reject the lie that says, "I will be happy when…" If contentment is your goal then you have to find a way of being content now, as you are. In this chapter I've suggested all sorts of practical ways in which our approach to life and our wider circle of relationships can help us keep a sense of balance and perspective and help us find contentment. I hope I have helped you put aside the notion that life would be so much better if only you could be instantly transported into a more acceptable body. I've mostly concentrated on valuable tools, the importance of relationships and strategies that will help. But I can't leave it at that.

Everything I've offered so far will probably work, but it will work especially well if you have a stable home, some solid friendships, enough intelligence to work out you've got a problem and enough resolve to want to change. Not everyone has these resources but those that do can probably manage to get by very nicely with the advice in this chapter. The irony is that when life is reasonably good we don't go looking for the best. We don't wonder if there is more. We are possibly less likely to look for God. Quite often it is those who realize the poverty of their own resources who more quickly grasp the offer of spiritual power. Does that make God a prop for the weak? Or a reality overlooked by the reasonably comfortable? I've suggested that living life loved is the key to self-confidence, so it's to that possibility we now turn our attention.

NOTES

1. All statistics in this section are from Anorexia, Bulimia Care (ABC), a registered UK charity supporting those with eating disorders and their carers: www.anorexiabulimiacare.co.uk

2. Janet Treasure, *Breaking Free from Anorexia Nervosa: A Survival Guide for Families, Friends and Suffers*, London: Psychology Press, 1997.

3. From the BEAT (Beating Eating Disorders) website: www.b-eat.co.uk

4. Nic Fleming, *Daily Telegraph*, January 2007, quoting research published in *Journal of Epidemiology and Community Health*.

Chapter 9

Live Life Loved

We started this book with the word "perfect", as in, "Perfect? Me? You've got to be kidding!"

It is a strange irony that while we none of us will admit to perfection, all of us think we have a fair idea of what it would look like. In the survey I carried out whilst researching for this book, I asked each person the questions: "What size are you now?" and "What size would you like to be?" With very few exceptions and regardless of their original size, the vast majority of women questioned said they wanted to be smaller than they actually were. Without having seen most of them, I can't even tell you if this was a reasonable aspiration.

Finally I asked one woman in her mid-fifties the same two questions. She said she was a size 12 but, refusing my agenda, she gave her own response to the second question: she said she wanted to be "content".

And probably some of you are thinking, "That's all right for her to say – I'd be content too if I was a size 12!" But this lady had her challenges. She admitted that failing eyesight and getting older were frustrations for her, but she still aspired to be content. It struck me that a character trait is a far more appealing description of a person than a dress size. As definitions go, words like "friendly", "amiable", "supportive", "funny", "considerate", "enthusiastic", "hard-working" or "content" feel a lot more attractive than a set of figures denoting size or weight. Yet many women do allow the numbers on their bathroom scales to determine their sense of emotional well-being. This isn't quite as mad as it sounds when you realize that it isn't just the fact or fear of being overweight that bothers them so much as the deeply held belief they hold – the one that says, "To be fat is to have failed."

They might have got this message from a parent or they might have succumbed to the media messages which tell us that having the perfect face or a well-toned, slim-sized body are simply matters of effort. Therefore if we haven't achieved these goals then we have only ourselves to blame, we are lazy or we lack self-discipline. In other words, we have failed. But do you remember what I told you about the recidivism rate of diets? That 95 per cent of all dieters will put the weight back on? This makes weight a statistical fact; it is neither a personal failure nor a character flaw but the culture we live in sure does make it feel that way.

If we are going to learn to love our bodies, we need to think differently about size and acceptability. Self-loathing is not a good place to start a programme of self-improvement.

If you are going to define success only in terms of appearance or size, then the reality is you might always be disappointed or even if you "fix" your problem using either huge amounts of determination or large sums of money, then your inner discontent may simply settle on the next thing that needs "sorting": the size of your house, your boring job, the weaknesses in your spouse. Discontentment is a very poor motive for change; it will never be satisfied. The quality that we need in order to live positively in a negative world is contentment and we need to find that quality now, as we are, with all our imperfections or shortcomings. We should not assume it will descend on us from on high once we've completely made ourselves over. By "contentment" I do not mean developing an attitude of complacency that's somewhere close to resignation. I mean a far more active attitude which allows us to live in a place of joy and self-acceptance even when things are a very long way from how we'd like them to be.

This kind of contentment is not simply a personality trait that would enhance your life in some rather spiritual-sounding way and make you a nicer person. Quite the opposite. As I've already said, I think learning to be content is a survival skill more akin to putting on a piece of armour.

So how do you find it? I believe the source or foundation for this contented attitude is the presence of unconditional love somewhere in your life.

Unconditional love

The word "love" comes so loaded with layers of meaning that sometimes psychologists prefer to avoid it. Instead they use the term "unconditional positive regard" which leaves love out of it altogether. Either way, what I'm getting at is having someone in your life who knows you with all your faults and failings yet also accepts you and loves you. This unconditional love is not related to your size, status, significance. The clue is in the wording: unconditional – that is, without conditions attached!

Unconditional love might come from a romantic source, although romantic love, especially in the early stages, is more often layered with unrealistic expectations. As we emphasized in the previous chapter, unconditional love can come from a parent, a sibling, a friend or a counsellor. The Bible gives a great definition of what unconditional love looks like and how it behaves:

> Love is patient, love is kind. It does not envy, it does not boast, it is
> not proud. It is not rude, it is not self-seeking, it is not easily angered,
> it keeps no record of wrongs. Love does not delight in evil but rejoices
> with the truth. It always protects, always hopes, always perseveres.[1]

Although the source of this love is not specified in this passage, the Greek word used is *agápè*, which is something different from *eros* (sexual/romantic love). So where do you go to find this kind of love?

Generally people look in one of three places: inside, alongside or outside.

Looking inside

According to Whitney Houston, in the song she made famous, learning to love yourself "is the greatest love of all".[2] Is there any truth in that idea? I'm not sure if it's the "greatest", but for many people it's the hardest because we are our own worst critics. We also feel uncomfortable with the idea of loving ourselves. It seems a bit narcissistic and requires not just self-belief but possibly self-centredness as well. People who look inside themselves subscribe to the notion that they only have themselves to rely on. This is a notion that appeals to our egos; it encourages us to dig deep to find inner reserves, to "search for the hero inside yourself", as M People put it in their memorable song. It says that if only we are brave enough, bold enough, determined enough, we will always succeed. However, this is an illusion; we do not always succeed. Not everything is possible because not everything is in our power. We may get the grades but not the job. And no amount of skill, learning or self-confidence can protect us from the random and distressing events that can totally derail our lives – such as getting cancer or being run over by a bus. We are not as in control of life as we'd like to think we are. Consequently it can feel pretty lonely being told that we only have our own resources to fall back on.

If the solution for self-doubt, inadequacy, discouragement, self-loathing or despair is to look yourself in the mirror and tell yourself firmly that you are wonderful, I'm not sure it'll work. Does anyone else notice the similarity between this activity and pulling yourself off the ground by your bootstraps? It can't actually be done and anyway, people with all those negative feelings very rarely look into mirrors. It's not that you are not wonderful (I've spent half this book trying to convince you that you are!). I do totally believe that human beings have a miraculous potential way beyond their physical components, but it's still not always possible to talk ourselves out of the dark places we sometimes inhabit.

Looking alongside

So the next thing we do when we know we need courage or self-belief is to look to someone else to provide it for us. If you've ever watched a child learning to ride a bike you'll appreciate the value of stabilizers. A good friend is a lot like a stabilizer. He or she will stop you from actually falling over as you wobble wildly from one side to the other. Ideally your parents should have been the first people in your life who acted in this capacity. I don't mean teaching you to ride a bike, I mean pouring enough love, affection and security into your life so that you grew up with an inner core of self-confidence, the courage to try new things and the resilience to pick yourself up again if you failed. Not everyone had the flying start that this kind of parenting can give, and that is another factor that was completely beyond your control. In fact growing up without this positive input is one of the hardest things from which to recover. Negative messages from parents are ingrained very deeply and feel more devastating than negative messages from anyone else. Recovery from this is a slow, slow process involving many factors, one of which will be the presence of other, positive people in your life.

All of us spend most of our lives "looking alongside" whenever we become aware of our own lack of resources, and there is nothing wrong with this. Every person in your life who accepts you for who you are, who encourages you when you feel disheartened, who is able to express a belief in your ability or restore your perspective when life seems out of control, is treasure and a gift. If you have any more than a handful of such people in your life you are fortunate indeed.

"No man is an island", yet in our individualistic society being seen to need other people is made to seem like a weakness, but I think we were made to "lean". Over the years I have leaned on other people's faith when my own has felt weak, I've leaned on other people's enthusiasm, I've leaned on other people's skill and I've leaned on other people's pockets! Why does that all sound so pathetic? Maybe because leaning sounds like the very opposite of standing on your own two feet, a value we rate very highly. Let me put it another way: other people's faith has encouraged me, other people's joy has lifted me, I've relied on other people's skill and I've benefited from other people's generosity. There now, I don't sound half so feeble! But the reality is the same: I am and always will be partly made up from what other people have put into me: courage, knowledge, kindness. I was never meant to live alone, I am meant to be in a "community", whether that's a set of friendships, a family, or a church.

So there is nothing wrong with looking alongside when you are looking for inner contentment. I know I said this in the previous chapter, but I think it bears repeating: there is a drawback. Other people are as fallible and needy as you are. Other people will sooner or later let you down: they will fail to be there for you in whatever way you needed them. They might misunderstand you. They might move away. They might just get busy with other stuff. No other individual can totally and reliably supply all that we need, and once we accept that fact our relationships will be greatly improved, we will be freed from a tendency to be either demanding or dependent, both of which will scare away the very people we feel we need.

Sometimes a needy person will find a person who "needs to be needed" and this can look like a mutually beneficial relationship, but it is not healthy, as the needy person is never free to outgrow their neediness because the person who "needs to be needed" needs them to stay needy. You might need to re-read that sentence but basically I'm saying that none of us are completely able to love without taking our own needs into account.

Someone much wiser than I has said that "there are endless 'ifs' hidden in the world's love".[3] What he meant was that people will love us *if* we are lovable, *if* we are beautiful, intelligent, successful or wealthy. Sometimes they will love us *if* we go along with their agenda or sometimes they will love us *if* they have the time and inclination. When we look alongside, we are at the mercy of other people. Effectively we give them power to dictate how we feel. If they like us we feel good, if they overlook us we feel gutted. But we don't have to give them that power, we don't have to pin our self-belief to a shaky source, nor do we have to fall back on the first strategy of self-reliance. There is a third option.

Looking outside

Looking outside might sound like a strange way to describe forming a relationship with God, but I want to emphasize that God is an external reality. Looking outside is not simply another version of the first option where you are left to search for the divinity within you. The God I mean is THE God, the one who if he is indeed real and exists, does so regardless of whether or not you believe in him. If I'm looking outside of myself for help, then I want it to come from someone beyond me, someone bigger than me, more powerful, someone who has the resources I am clearly lacking. I don't want to be alone, just going round and round in my head with my own view of things. I want someone who can give me a better view of things. As I have got to know God, I have learnt what he thinks about me and it is this view that is so important.

God's existence can't be proved but I believe he can be found. If we could prove he was there, then no one would have a choice about whether or not to believe in him, which would be pretty terrible really – a bit like living under a spiritual dictatorship. In other words, God hides because it's more fun to be found than to force his presence on us – but he doesn't hide very well. There are "toes" that pop out beneath the curtain or "fingers" that can be seen around the wardrobe door. He isn't that hard to find if you're looking. The Bible says, "You will seek and find me when you seek me with all your heart",[4] and Jesus promised, "Seek and you will find".[5] There is plenty of evidence around if you are willing to consider it: the universe, the laws that govern it, your own amazingly complex body, your ability to comprehend the world and the peculiar fact of your own conscience. Not everyone takes an intellectual approach to the question of whether or not God is real, and an intuitive approach can work just as well. We can begin to see his presence in other people and open our own lives to his influence by simply praying, "God, if you're there, I'd like to find you."

(By the way, don't let the pronoun "he" put you off. God is neither he nor she. Putting a gender on God is like trying to assign a colour to the wind. The wind is neither blue nor red; it is not defined by colour. God is neither male nor female; he is not defined by gender. Because human beings were created in his image we can assume his nature encompasses both male and female traits, as we would define them. God is not a he or a she but neither is "he" an "it". He is personal – that's why we use a pronoun and due to the constraints of our language and our culture, it happens to be a male pronoun.)

As I've said, it's what God says he thinks about me, the view from where he is standing, that makes all the difference to how I see myself. I don't see myself clearly and realistically; I need to look at myself through someone else's eyes to get a clearer picture.

Remember the moment in most makeover shows when the individual hoping to be transformed is made to come face to face with how they see themselves now? Sometimes they are made to stand in a 360-degree mirror or sometimes they are asked to rank themselves in terms of size with a line of women. We know they are going to get it wrong; they will overestimate their size or they will experience distress out of all proportion to their problem. Jesus said something which gives an amazing insight into what's going on at this moment. He said, "Your eye is the lamp of your body. When your eyes are good, your whole body is full of light. But when they are bad your body is also full of darkness."[6] When our "eyes" are not good, when we see ourselves as faulty, our whole body is "full of darkness" or repugnant to us. What we need is to stand outside of ourselves to get a better perspective.

Greg Ferguson wrote a song called "If I Could See Through Your Eyes", wanting to see what God sees when he sees us and speculating that it would be very different from the way we see ourselves.

If I could look through your eyes…
I would see that I am precious
I would know that I am prized…
If I could look through your eyes.[7]

If I see myself the way God sees me, then I cannot say that I am a misfit, a mistake or a meaningless person, because he does not see me that way. How much easier it feels to take those words into our mouths. Now try saying that you are precious and prized. These words can feel as awkward in your mouth as the word "perfect"!

Yet if you are going to find contentment you are going to need some new words to describe yourself. I'd like to give you three. I'm not plucking these words out of the air because they sound good; I'm using them because they accurately reflect God's stated opinion of you. This is what God thinks of you.

I'd like to invite you to take each word and mull it over. Imagine each word is a stone that you have picked up while walking along a beautiful blustery beach. Put each one in a pocket of your mind, take it out from time to time and ask yourself what difference it would make if this word applied to you. If you really want to "own" the word, write it on an actual pebble (white nail varnish works well) and keep it in a real pocket. On my study desk, I have these words on actual stones. They fit in the palm of my hand and I sometimes hold them when I pray. This might sound like a strange thing to do, and certainly a few years ago, when I was given a stone on a retreat day and told to let it "speak" to me, I disgraced myself with giggling and the stone was predictably silent! Back then I hadn't really got the hang of meditation. Now I know the object (a stone or a cross or a candle) is simply a means to help you talk to God. So as I talk to God or simply sit and listen, the weight of the stones helps impress the words in my heart. They are a silent witness to how he feels about me. Here's the first word:

Chosen

I am "chosen". If we are really honest, this is not a word we are comfortable with, for two reasons. One, we are frightened we might not be chosen.

" We just want you to imagine..."

"Imagine each word is a stone" (p.179)

Many of us have never recovered from those moments in PE lessons when it became painfully obvious no one wanted us on their team. Secondly, "chosen" implies selection; it has overtones of superiority; being "chosen" sounds rather presumptuous and self-inflated. Countless groups of people down the centuries have declared themselves to be "the chosen ones" in a way that has included the "faithful" and excluded everyone else.

So being chosen is a difficult concept. It's a bit like the idea of winning and losing. Some schools have outlawed sports days because it's too distressing to say to someone, "You are the winner" because then you are saying to someone else, "You are the loser". I love the story about a school sports day with a difference. It's one of those slightly mushy stories told on the internet but there's no reason to suppose it's not true and even if it isn't, it still makes the point beautifully as a kind of parable. The school in question was a special needs school. When sports day came round a small group of children lined up at the start line, some with Down's Syndrome, some with other disabilities. The whistle blew and all the children set off towards the finishing line. But with only 20 yards to go, one little girl fell over and began to wail over the scrape down her knee. One by one all the others stopped and turned around. Then one by one they all came back to their fallen classmate, patted her, helped her up and said nice things. Finally, encouraged no doubt by their teachers, they remembered they were meant to be crossing the finishing line, so they all held hands and walked across together with beaming smiles on their faces.

Did those children understand the concept of winning? Part of me wants to say, "No they didn't" but another part of me wants to shout "Yes!" They really did understand about winning; they understood that we can all be winners.

God has the same approach when it comes to the concept of choosing. He chooses everyone! For us the word "chosen" implies "selection" – in other words, some people being left out. For God, the word "chosen" implies "invited" and everyone is invited! If you don't believe me, check it out.[8] So if you are not comfortable with the word "chosen", say to yourself, "I am invited", because the Bible makes it clear that everyone is invited to know him – there is no one excluded. Even those who've never heard of him can discern him in creation. God chooses to put everyone on his invitation list to life. As William P. Young said in his bestselling book *The Shack*, there is a way in which God can look at each one of us and say, "I am especially fond of you."[9] It's not that God has favourites, but he has favourite reasons why he is especially fond of you.

Intriguingly, Jesus also said to his disciples, "You did not choose me but I chose you", which makes it clear that becoming a Christian is not entirely based on my own choice (although our choice does come into it); it is being pursued, sought out and invited by the one who has known us personally since before the beginning of time.[10]

When my children were small one of our favourite story books was called *Before I Was a Kid*.[11] It is the account of a conversation between a mother and her small child, and the child starts by asking Mummy, "Before I was a kid, what was I?" They go back through the stages of life – toddler, baby, infant, foetus and embryo – with the child asking each time, "And before that?" Tantalizingly, the final question the child asks is, "Before I was an embryo, what was I?" The final page in the story gives the most simple yet profound answer to one of life's most important questions. The Mummy says, "You were a person in the mind of God." He had you in mind; you are neither a repetition nor an aberration, and you are not an accident. You are a planned person; God knew you in advance and brought you into being on purpose.

Are you beginning to see what a difference this word "chosen" can make to how you see yourself?

Cherished

Being "cherished" is not a regular nine-to-five experience for most of us. Being overworked, being belittled, being overlooked, being bored – all of these we can probably relate to, but being cherished may feel a little outside our experience. My dictionary tells me it means "to protect or tend lovingly, to value". If I am cherished, then I am valued, but not in the monetary sense of that word.

If you are married you made a commitment to "cherish". In case you've forgotten, it was right there in the line before "Till death us do part". A while back I read a letter from a wife to an agony aunt column in a national newspaper. She clearly didn't feel cherished. She was older than her husband, they had had three children and she described herself as having a few "floppy bits" and grey hair while her husband still looked fit and youthful. She had begun to eat blueberries with wild green algae with yoghurt for breakfast; what else would the columnist recommend? I was reassured to read the advice that only fish should eat algae. I was slightly disconcerted that she was advised to dye her hair (after all, grey might suit her) and utterly appalled by the columnist's final comment that she should pay a surgeon to suck up all the flab. After all, "I know these things are not as important as having a beautiful soul but we live in a time where everything is a commodity and we know where those are going: down, down, down."

Excuse me? A commodity? A life partner, a precious wife, a woman who has brought three children into the world. A commodity? What a horrible way to be described. Here is a person who should be cherished. There is a verse in Proverbs that says, "A wife of noble character who can find? She is worth more than rubies."[12] Whether you call it a "beautiful soul" or a "noble character", what is clear in this verse is that it is not your outward appearance that determines your worth. Don't feel left out by this verse if you are not a wife; you can substitute "sister of noble character" or "friend of noble character". The point is still the same: who you are matters heaps more than what you look like.

The reality is that I'm cherished by God not because I look good. I'm not even valued for my skills or abilities, which is just as well, as not all of us are gifted. I am cherished simply because I am.

Dawn French, a British comedienne who describes herself as "51 and almost completely spherical", writes movingly in her autobiography of a conversation she had with her father when she was about thirteen. As she was about to go out to a party wearing bright purple suede hot pants and a slightly see-through cheesecloth top, her father took her to one side. Instead of the stern parental lecture that she was expecting, he told her she looked stunning. He told her how much he loved and adored her, that she was a "rare thing, an uncommon beauty, a dazzling, exquisite, splendid young woman". He also said that the boys "should fight tournaments to win her affection" and that she was utterly deserving of the very best. She recalls that she went off to the party "feeling ten foot tall and fabulous". Who wouldn't? What a brilliant Dad! So many years later she describes that conversation as being given her "armour".

Not everyone had a parent who gave them that gift of self-belief. This one conversation with her father lasted her a lifetime (her father died when she was nineteen). If one such conversation can do so much good, then it's easy to see that a steady stream of negative remarks could also leave a devastating trail of negativity that would last a lifetime. I would like you to know that you have a heavenly Father who wants to put his hands lovingly on your shoulders, look you in the eye and tell you, "You are gorgeous." He also wants you to know that you mean the world to him, that he loves you "truly, madly and deeply", and he wants the best for you. He has wept over and been outraged by those things that have harmed you and he longs for you to come close enough to know how much he loves you. The Bible is full of pictures, stories and parables that try to express how much God loves us, from the direct "You are precious and honoured in my sight and I love you",[13] to a sublime image of a father singing over an infant: "The Lord takes great delight in you, he will quiet you with his love, he will rejoice over you with singing."[14] Jesus told so many stories about the Father's extravagant love. In the story of the Prodigal Son, the father sets aside all dignity to run to greet his wayward boy, even though all his wealth has been squandered and the child is completely undeserving. In the story of the Lost Sheep, the shepherd doesn't settle for the ninety-nine sheep he has but sets out to look for the one that wandered.

Greater than all the stories Jesus told, nothing speaks louder than the cross. That God himself, in Jesus, should submit to all the rejection and cruelty his creatures could throw at him and through this astonishing act of self-giving open a way for us to become the "children of God".[15] You can examine the cross from every angle but until you experience it as God's demonstration of his total commitment to you, you will not realize that it was all about love.

So just how do you experience God's love? How do you start a relationship with God if you've never had one before? The Bible describes becoming a Christian as taking a step of "spoken belief". Paul, the apostle, says there are two things you need to do: "believe in your heart" and "speak with your mouth".[16] The believing part might be private and can begin with a prayer as simple as, "God, I want to invite you into my life." The spoken part implies that you are prepared to go public in your search, prepared to be known as a Christian. This most probably means joining a group, a church, finding a way to worship and express your faith publicly. It's this public identification with other Christians that often takes people from a rather uncertain "I think I'm a Christian" to a more confident "I'm sure I'm Christian".

A relationship with God is no different from human relationships in the sense that it takes time to build up the trust and confidence you have from knowing someone well. Believing that God loves you is a bit like wading into the sea. At the outset you are only prepared to paddle, to get your feet wet. If you want to experience more of God's love you have to wade out deeper, possibly out of your depth, and trust yourself to the current. Paul prayed that

Christians might know "how wide, and long and high and deep is the love of Christ", a love that he admitted "surpasses knowledge". I'm driven to using a metaphor because it's hard to put into concrete terms what it means to feel cherished by God, but that doesn't mean to say it's an abstract or theoretical relationship. This is a reality which has a definite outcome in terms of joy and confidence.

Let me try to give you an example of a way in which knowing God loves me makes a difference. This story might sound far too trivial to be "proof"; I only offer it as an example. Earlier this year I was caught up in an emergency with my son. He had been saving and planning for his gap year travel for over two years. Two days before he was due to depart, an acute medical issue cropped up which threatened to ruin all his plans. In the middle of a midnight dash to hospital, my son commented that I seemed very calm. He knows his mother saves hysteria for silly things, so my aura of "icy calm" had alerted him to the fact that we were potentially facing a big problem! I said I was calm because there was no point getting in a state until we knew the worst, but privately I didn't feel at all confident. In fact I turned on the car radio to distract us both, only to hear a singer on a secular station crooning to me that "God's eye is on the sparrow", a line Jesus said to remind us just how valuable we are to God. It was hilarious. In the middle of all that anxiety, I laughed out loud. If God could keep an eye on the birds, he hadn't taken his eyes off me. I had tried to turn away and distract myself, but God had spoken to me through a song on the radio at the precise moment I needed to hear it, finding a way to comfort me and remind me that no amount of worry would separate me from him. My son's condition didn't improve immediately and I had to leave him in hospital awaiting surgery, with all his plans in tatters. I drove home hoping that God still knew the score and trusting him that it was all going to be OK. By the next morning the crisis, amazingly, had passed and my son made his flight after all.

Many Christians could tell you many similar stories of times when they have "heard" the voice of God. This year alone I have "heard'" God in a rainbow that appeared at a moment of acute fear; through a novel that moved me deeply when I was feeling very low; and countless times through prayers, services or readings. One of my favourite definitions of what it means to be cherished by God is given by Gerald O'Mahony, a Catholic priest who wrote a book called *Finding the Still Point*:

God loves me with an everlasting, unshakeable, unbreakable love. Nothing I could do will stop him from loving me. He loves me as a Father; he loves me not because I am a good child but because I am his child. He loves me with a love that has no strings attached to it. He has loved me since before time began and will still love me after the end of time. No power of self-destruction within me is stronger than God's love for me. All that I have to do is trust in his love for me, since he is incurably friendly. I am worthwhile as a person and I cannot lose my worth because it does not depend on me in the first place but on a lover who never changes.[17]

"A lover who never changes" – what a wonderful description of the one person I need to lead me to a place of contentment. The idea of change brings me to my final word.

Changed

Throughout the whole process of writing this book I have been aware that my message has been slightly schizophrenic. On the one hand I have been encouraging you to feel great about yourself, whatever your size and shape; and on the other hand I have been dishing out advice about how to change your size and shape! Am I just confused?

I hope not. And I hope I haven't confused you either. Basically I'm more than happy for anyone to improve their diet, change their shape and enhance their appearance, but only if they do so for the right reasons. Rather than bully people into simply making more of an effort with their appearance, I've wanted to help women find their intrinsic value and then express that in their lifestyle.

It's not been a book about self-improvement, although, goodness knows, you may well have found it shelved in that section of the bookstore. I don't really believe in self-improvement; it rather smacks of self-reliance. I believe there are lots of superficial surface rearrangements you can make that will go a long way, but I also believe that we were not meant to be self-reliant, that God wants us to rely on him to change us from the inside out. The word "changed" reminds me that although God loves me as I am, "warts and all", I do not have to stay that way. It also reminds me that the most important ways I have to change, I cannot do for myself. The Bible teaches us very clearly that we cannot impress God. No amount of surface rearrangements or clever dressing is going to deal with a resentment issue that poisons a relationship I might have. No amount of make-up will cover up the guilt I feel over something I did wrong or the anxiety I can't shake off. An exercise programme will probably help me overcome an addiction, but it won't reveal the cause of my addiction, and if I skip on my exercise routine I might fall prey to the same addiction.

If we really want to change, and probably most of us do in some way or another, there is only one way, and that is to admit we are not the person we would like to be. The Bible calls this admission of helplessness "conviction of sin". It is the point of admitting that we can't put right all the wrong stuff in our lives, and it is one of the first steps towards becoming a Christian, although admitting we can't fix things on our own is just as important a step even if we are already a Christian. Christianity is not about self-improvement, it's all about what God does in us, and the first thing he does is forgive us, and then he changes our outlook gradually over time. His presence in our lives, his Holy Spirit, will cause "fruit" to grow: "love, joy, peace, patience, kindness, goodness, faithfulness, gentleness and self-control".[18] These are the kind of qualities that I would prefer to define my life, rather than my size or shape or appearance.

God does love us exactly how we are, whether we are a heap of insecurities or a boiling cauldron of rage, but he also expects us to change, and he does give us the power to change if we are willing to work with him. Even though he loves us, he sees how our fear, anger, guilt or self-destructive habits limit who were meant to be. He wants to help us change.

I think maybe "changing" would be a better word than "changed", because I will always be a work in progress, still so far off becoming the best that I can be. Often when I get frustrated with myself and think I haven't changed much or that there's not much Christian character to be seen in me, I have to go back to the first two words. I know I can more easily be changed when I've allowed the words "chosen" and "cherished" to become deeply embedded in my life. When I look outside of myself and accept God's invitation to a life in relationship with him, then he promises to give me the power to change. The Bible talks about this change in terms of beauty instead of ashes; a radiant face, not an anxious outlook; a purposeful life, not a meaningless existence.

Christianity is both inspirational and aspirational. In other words it is comforting (God loves you as you are) *and* it is challenging (God wants you make the best of yourself). You need to take on board the first statement in brackets before you can set about the second. However, one final point I'd like to make is that I am uncomfortably aware that I may be making this process of inner transformation sound simple. I'd like to emphasize that learning to love and learning to be loved (by God or anyone else for that matter) is a journey. It isn't easy and it isn't instant. If you have been a Christian for a long time you may be thinking to yourself, "I know all that about God loving me in my head, but I still feel bad, it hasn't reached my heart. What else do I need? Better theology, more Bible knowledge, prayer ministry or counseling?" Maybe all of those things would be helpful, but the point I'd like to make is that correct theology and memory verses are rarely enough. Transformation happens when we experience "life" (just the everyday ups and downs, the good, bad and indifferent stuff we live through) and it happens over time. I do not mean by this that it has to take a "lifetime", but I do not want to mislead you into thinking there is one simple spiritual solution that will bring about instant transformation.

What I am trying to say is that there are so many factors and all of them together will bring about transformation. In this book I have encouraged you to:

- Go on a diet, change your wardrobe and take up exercise; in other words, do something to actively change your situation.
- Celebrate your body in the way you care for it and speak about it.
- Challenge the negative self-talk that goes through your head.
- Develop deep friendships so that you can learn to receive acceptance, compliments and appreciation naturally.
- Be honest with yourself about what originally caused you to feel so bad.
- Be patient with yourself as you change.
- Look outside yourself to the God who created you and loves you.

Personal transformation is like a complex recipe with many ingredients. Not only do you have to combine all these factors; you also have to allow time – time for "the yeast" to rise, time for the finished article to cook. Deep-down change is rarely instant. It is a journey we are on for all our lives. A Chinese proverb reminds us that "The longest journey begins with the first step." So long as you are going in the right direction, be patient with yourself. One day you will look back and be able to say, "Look how far I've come!"

I have used the title *How to Feel Good Naked* as both a hook to catch your interest and as homage to Gok Wan, whose joyful affirmation of women of all sizes has been hugely positive. I deliberately chose the word *feel* because I've put the focus on your inner state of mind and your beliefs rather than merely on how you look from the outside. However, I'm not entirely comfortable with the idea of leaving you naked! This isn't prudishness on my part; the issue is that in the Bible nudity is almost always a symbol of shame or destitution. And that's the last thing I would want to leave you feeling. I would like instead to leave you clothed. Clothing in the Bible is richly symbolic of status and value. Clothing speaks about dignity and honour. Even God wears clothes. He wears creation like a garment. It may only be a metaphorical garment on an invisible, transcendent God, but the image means that God is clothed in glory, the beauty of his creation – its variety, diversity and complexity speak loudly about the kind of God he is.

So it's hardly surprising that God wants to "clothe" you. And here is the wardrobe he is offering, in words written by the apostle Paul:

> So, chosen by God for this new life of love, dress in the wardrobe God picked out for you: compassion, kindness, humility, quiet strength, discipline… whatever else you put on, wear love. It's your basic all-purpose garment. Never be without it.[19]

Did you notice that word "chosen" again? Having a wardrobe "picked out for you" is surely a way to be "cherished". We are told to wear love, "your basic all-purpose garment". There are two ways of understanding that phrase, to "wear love": either you should love others all the time or you should know you are loved all the time. So many people try the former before they've grasped the latter, and it's pretty difficult. Instead you have to wear love because love is the covering God has given you, the forgiveness for all the things you wish you'd never done, the covering for everything and anything for which you feel ashamed.

Being loved will bring you to a place of contentment. Being contented will help you feel at home in the amazing body you've got.

Be imitators of God, therefore, as dearly loved children and *live a life of love.*[20]

To be free from our self-conscious hang-ups, to be happy in our skin, to be joyful about who we are, to *really* "feel good naked", we need to
Live...
    life...
        loved.

Notes

1. 1 Corinthians 13:4–7.
2. 'The Greatest Love of All', written by Michael Masser and Linda Creed, originally recorded by George Benson for the 1977 Mohammed Ali film, *The Greatest*.
3. Henri Nouwen, *The Return of the Prodigal Son*, London: Darton, Longman and Todd, 1992.
4. Jeremiah 29:13.
5. Matthew 7:7.
6. Luke 11:34.
7. Greg Ferguson, 'Ever Devoted', Willow Creek Community Church, 1989.
8. 2 Peter 3:9; Matthew 22:8–9.
9. William P. Young, *The Shack*, London: Hodder and Stoughton, 2008.
10. See Ephesians 1:4 and Psalm 139.
11. Rita Spears-Stewart, *Before I was a Kid*, USA: Pacific Press, 1991.
12. Proverbs 31:10.
13. Isaiah 43:4.
14. Zephaniah 3:17.
15. 1 John 3:1.
16. Romans 10:9.
17. G. O'Mahony, *Finding the Still Point*, Westbury: Eagle Publishing, 1992.
18. Galatians 5:22.
19. Colossians 3:12–14 from *The Message* by Eugene Peterson.
20. Ephesians 5:2 (emphasis mine).

Resources

www.anybody.squarespace.com
This website describes its purpose as "giving women a voice to challenge the limited physical representation of females in contemporary society". There are a wide-range of articles on the subject of body image.

www.thesite.org
TheSite.org is owned and run by YouthNet UK, a registered charity. It aims to be the first place all young adults turn to when they need support and guidance through life. It provides factsheets and information and has a large section on health and well-being. It also has a helpful list of organisations offering national helplines.

www.campaignforrealbeauty.com
Although this is an advertising site for beauty products it also contains some excellent videos notably *Evolution* which shows how a very plain girl is transformed into a glamorous model and *Onslaught* which is about how advertising affects young girls. The Dove Global Report into how women see themselves, dated 2004, also makes interesting reading.

www.ingenious.org.uk
The Read section of this website has interesting articles relating science and culture, in particular there are interesting sections on women's health and on body image.

www.b-eat.co.uk
Beat is the leading UK charity for people with eating disorders and their families, it is the working name of the Eating Disorders Association. They provide help lines, online support and a network of self-help groups.

www.anorexiabulimiacare.co.uk
ABC is a small "but passionate" UK charity that offers help and support to individuals and families affected by eating related issues. They produce resources and offer a befriending service whereby people who have been through an eating

disorder are linked up with a sufferer to offer support and encouragement. They also offer "Ache", a parent support line offering confidential support and advice.

Obviously there are many experts out there in the field of colour analysis and style consultation. My particular appreciation goes to these two who have inspired me personally:

www.lavishladies.co.uk
This is a website run Alison Tinsley who offered many helpful suggestions for the chapter on self-presentation. Alison can offer you a colour confidence session or a style consultation of the type discussed.

www.janefardon.com
Jane Fardon is an image consultant who has designed her own range of high quality cosmetics which offer very good value for money and are based on colour analysis.

To follow the book's progress, leave feedback or see Sheila's speaking dates, see this page on Facebook:
http://www.facebook.com/howtofeel

For more information about Sheila's other books or to read her blog go to **www.sheilabridge.com**